African American History

A Captivating Guide to the People and Events that Shaped the History of the United States

Free Bonus from Captivating History (Available for a Limited time)

Hi History Lovers!

Now you have a chance to join our exclusive history list so you can get your first history ebook for free as well as discounts and a potential to get more history books for free! Simply visit the link below to join.

Captivatinghistory.com/ebook

Also, make sure to follow us on:

Twitter: @Captivhistory

Facebook: Captivating History: @captivatinghistory

Contents

Part 1: The American Revolution Through the American Civil War

Introduction

The history of African Americans is a long and tragic chronicle of events. The people who dared to stand up and speak out against the systemic cruelty and oppression were often brutally killed for their efforts. This has created a rich tapestry of defiant and courageous leaders and followers who have gradually pressed for the evolution of thought within the United States of America.

Between the sixteenth and nineteenth centuries, African Americans struggled to be recognized as more than just the possessions of slave owners. The strange dichotomy between the free African Americans being treated as people while at the same time the slaves were treated as property helped to open the eyes of numerous Americans to the inherent problems with slavery. Even as the country was being established, some of the founding fathers spoke out against slavery, recognizing it to be at least as oppressive as the tyranny they were fighting against. However, they were willing to sacrifice this belief to gain the support of the Southern colonies against the British. This compromise would fester over the next hundred years, becoming one of the primary causes of the American Civil War. While there were other reasons for the war, it is impossible (or at least very irresponsible) to fail to acknowledge that slavery was one of the main drivers.

Following the emancipation of slaves at the end of the American Civil War, the country struggled with treating those of African heritage as being equal to those of European ancestry. Both the Northern and Southern States generally treated an entire race as second-class citizens because of the inherent bias established in the early days of the colonies. It was only after the Civil Rights Movement that African Americans could finally force politicians and court systems to acknowledge the rights that were often denied them based solely on their heritage.

Ultimately, the tone and treatment of African Americans were set during the early days of the colonies. When it became apparent that owning slaves would be the quickest way to achieve prosperity, the people who journeyed to find new opportunity and a new life were willing to disregard the humanity of an entire race simply to achieve their own goals. To fully understand the problems African Americans face today, it is essential to understand how they were brought to this country and the conditions they lived under, both as slaves and as freemen. From the very beginning, those who came from Africa were treated differently than those colonists who reached North America from Europe.

Chapter 1 – The First Africans in America

The first people of African descent brought to North America were brought as slaves. Though it is possible that some people of African heritage arrived for other reasons, it is incredibly rare. From the beginning, Africans were taken from their homes and brought to the colonies to be slaves for the Colonials. The original slaves actually found freedom far earlier and joined the natives in living free off the land.

The First African Slaves on the Mainland

Spanish Colonials were the first to bring slaves to the New World. While they would enslave the indigenous people, they were also accustomed to abducting people in Africa and bringing them to a new land to work. This made it easier to control their slaves. Escape was more difficult since the Africans did not know the areas where they were brought to live. The explorers often chose to slaughter the indigenous people instead of running the risk of having them escape back to their tribes and freedom.

The first ship carrying African slaves to North America is believed to have arrived in 1526 with the Spanish Colonials who came to the New World with Lucas Vasquez de Ayllon. The slaves were brought to the small colony called San Miguel de Gualdape, a region that would later become the state of Georgia. In these early days, the Spanish did not imprison their slaves, so the Spanish slave laborers could escape from their captivity. They found assistance from the natives in the area and could make a living, free from the kind of labor that future slaves would endure. The slaves who were not fortunate enough to escape were relocated to Hispaniola following the death of the colony's leader, Ayllon.

The first Africans to reach the continent escaped and lived free in the New World, but many of the slaves that followed were less fortunate.

By the beginning of the seventeenth century, it was clear the land in North America was incredibly fertile, particularly in the Southern regions. European immigrants and government bodies from all of the colonizing countries saw the benefits of unpaid labor, so slavery spread throughout much of the newly settled areas in both North and South America. The highest concentrations of slaves were in areas where farming was the main industry, such as in the Southern colonies in North America and the Caribbean islands. This was true regardless of the country from which the settlers came. Though European countries did not always get along with each other, they usually had a certain level of respect for one another, largely because they viewed the value of other Europeans as being greater to those from Africa. Certain religions did not agree with the common outlook of the majority of Europeans, and it was proven early on that the natives of North America were far kinder toward the slaves. These religious grounds and the natives were the first to question the inherent flaws and logic that allowed for slavery. They did not believe that enslaving others because of perceived superiority was just common sense; they saw it as wrong.

The areas with the most fertile ground and ideal environment for crops were also those with the hottest climate and most affected by insects and disease. While this was not as severe in the Southern areas of North America as it was in the Caribbean Islands, it still resulted in slaves dying from heat exhaustion and inhumane environments. In the early days, the only incentive to treat slaves better was so slave owners would not have to spend as much money to replace them. In places like Saint-Domingue and Hispaniola (the modern-day countries of Haiti and the Dominican Republic), a large percentage of both slaves and colonists died from disease, such as yellow fever. In these regions, slaves were forced to work as much as possible under the assumption the slaves would not make it past the first year. Slave owners in the American colonies treated and fed their slaves a certain way in an attempt to permit them to live longer and hence produce for the owner. Slaves were viewed as property and slave owners worked their slaves less so they would last longer, including any children they would have. The different perspectives on slavery meant the overall experience of slaves varied based on their life expectancy. Slaves who were likely to increase a slaveholder's labor force would be treated slightly better than those who were not expected to live a year.

The First Documented Arrival

While slaves were brought to the continent prior to the early seventeenth century, the first documented shipment of Africans was brought over by the Dutch in 1619. There were 20 Africans aboard a ship that arrived at Jamestown, a British colony. Even in the early days, the promise of what could be earned from the tobacco trade had colonists looking for ways to increase production. Slaves were the perfect solution. Ironically, African Americans were as instrumental to the foundation of the country and its prosperity as any invention or governance by Europeans.

Without the contribution of African Americans, the New World would not have been nearly so successful. Indentured servants still came to the country, but their potential was not as lucrative or desirable because they were treated better than a slave. Perhaps the biggest disadvantage to bringing indentured servants to the colonies was they would eventually be free to make their own way. This meant those who brought them would spend money for the servants to come to the country, spend money on their training, and then lose that investment once the agreed-upon time of servitude was over. Slaves were more desirable for labor because these restrictions did not apply. The initial cost of the slave was the most obvious financial setback, but the return on that investment had the potential to be substantially more, even though the slave owner had to continue to pay for the basics to maintain the slave. This meant that any time and money put toward their slaves would be returned over the entire life of the slave. Compared to indentured servants, slavery was far more appealing, particularly on plantations requiring large numbers of laborers.

Following that first recorded shipment, Africans were brought over in droves. Some estimates report there could have been as many as seven million slaves brought over during the eighteenth century. Children of slaves became the property of the slave owners, and they could be traded or sold, making them a huge profit with very little cost. This further denied Africa the population and strong people it needed, setting the continent back even further. The ravages of slavers had a significantly negative impact on an entire continent as communities were decimated for the greed of European trade. Though the Spanish are often accused of being the most egregious offenders, the British were every bit as culpable. They created a highly efficient way of stealing lives from people in the name of profit.

The Triangle Trade

The Spanish and Portuguese may have a reputation today as being the most prolific slave traders. However, John Hawkins was actually an instrumental character in the slave trade between the sixteenth and nineteenth centuries. As a commander in the English navy, he helped to found the Triangle Trade.

As the name suggests, the Triangle Trade was conducted in three parts. Slave ships departed England to collect slaves from countries in the western part of Africa. They would attack villages and take villagers aboard the ships to be slaves in the Americas, just as the Spanish and Portuguese did. It was never a fair fight because the Africans did not have the same weaponry and were easily scared by the pistols and weapons the British wielded. Those who were taken were placed on ships, tearing families apart as the slavers often did not take children who were too young to fetch a good price and who were likely to die during the voyage.

Over time, the British decided this was less than desirable, so they turned to trading for slaves. They would bring goods from Britain to trade with the Africans in return for people. Usually, the people who were traded to the British belonged to slavers already on the continent.

The next stage was to bring the slaves to the New World. The enslaved Africans were brought across the Atlantic under some of the worst conditions. They were treated as cattle instead of people. Once they reached North America, the slaves were sold at auction. The British ships would fill the lower decks (that once held the slaves) with the crops from the Southern colonies and some goods from the Northern ones, and return to England.

Once they arrived back in British ports, the goods were sold, and the ship would return to Africa to begin the cycle again. New Englanders entered the Triangle Trade and sent goods and rum to Africa in exchange for slaves.

The British played an increasingly significant role in the slave trade as they continued to take over areas following wars and struggles with other countries. They would often insert themselves or take over from other slavers. Though they never cornered the market on African lives, the British played a large part in its advancement and continuation into the nineteenth century. Over the course of two hundred and forty-five years (the time when Hawkins began the British involvement in the trade), it is estimated the British initiated ten thousand voyages along the Triangle Trade. The estimated number of people transported over those ten thousand voyages was nearly three and a half million. The only country to have devastated more African lives was Portugal. The Portuguese were involved in the trade before the British and continued for about 50 years after the British abolished the practice of the slave trade. Hawkins made the first voyage under Queen Elizabeth 1 and involvement in the trade didn't cease until 1807, 30 years after the American Revolution.

A Complex View on Africans

Slavery was an institution built into the first governance of the colonies. The very first legal code drafted and enacted within the colonies was the Massachusetts Body of Liberties, which legalized slavery in Massachusetts in 1641. A stranger legal event occurred in Virginia in 1654 when people of African descent who were free were granted the right to be slaveholders themselves. However, the vast majority (if not almost all of them) of the slave purchases were made as a way of freeing family and friends from slavery. This means that less than 15 years after slavery was made legal, some of the colonies recognized the humanity of the slaves, although that recognition was not directly given.

Less than a decade after acknowledging the humanity of Africans, Virginia passed another law that ignored it. It ruled the children of slaves were also the property of the slaveholder, meaning these children would spend their lives enslaved. Following this ruling, a growing number of African women chose to attempt abortions rather than bring a child into such a terrible life.

Even from the early days, there were people who were staunchly against slavery for humanitarian reasons. The Quakers, a pacifist religious group, would not acknowledge any person as a slave. They did not hold to the convenience of the immoral trade and treatment of people, no matter how financially beneficial it was. There were few groups able to see the hypocrisy as easily as the Quakers because both Northern and Southern colonies had too much to lose by acknowledging there was a problem. After the indigenous people, groups like the Quakers treated Africans, and those of African descent, as equals while the colonies (and later the States) struggled to reconcile their views with the problems they created by acknowledging slaves as humans without treating them as such.

The Quakers were so opposed to slavery they passed their own laws in 1688. The Germantown Quaker Petition Against Slavery was the first law within the colonies that refused to recognize the institution of slavery. This was enacted and enforced in Pennsylvania, where the majority of Quakers resided.

In an attempt to determine the rights of Africans and their descendants, Virginia was the first to enact a law limiting their humanity in 1691. The law forbade any white person from marrying anyone outside of their own race. This type of discrimination was one of the oldest and staunchest holdouts against African Americans well into the twentieth century. All but a few States had laws on the books that forbade interracial marriages. A few States repealed the law before the twentieth century, but more than 50% of the country outlawed interracial marriages at the beginning of the 1900s.

By 1691, Virginia had developed a negative view of freeing slaves, believing it to be a high risk action. A freed slave would look for ways to free other slaves, potentially buying them from the market and creating a larger class of freed Africans. To stem the number of free slaves, Virginia passed a law limiting how many free slaves could live in the colony. Once a slave was freed, the former slave had six months to move out of the colony; they would not be allowed to stay near the plantation or family beyond those six months. This was an obvious hardship for the freed slaves, but the colony still feared the law did not do enough to dissuade the practice of freeing slaves . To ensure slave owners had their own incentive not to free slaves, the former master was responsible for paying for the freed slave to leave the colony.

Early Division in How Slaves Were Viewed
During the early days, slaves were used primarily on rice, tobacco, and indigo plantations. This meant they were far more common in the Southern territories than the Northern ones. While the North did rely on the work of slaves, they did not have the kind of contacts and connections to them as the plantation owners, lawyers, and people in the South. It was much easier for Northerners to see the oppression and to overlook the financial benefits they enjoyed because of slavery, even before the colonies turned against England.

Plantations were largely unsuccessful in the Northern colonies because the growing seasons were too short, the soil less fertile, and the environment less friendly for agriculture. Realizing they could not rely on agriculture, the Northern colonies turned to other means for their prosperity. This often took the form of industry, trade, and business. The Southern colonies were incredibly prosperous because of their crops, so they did not seek to find other means of making a living. Trade flowed easily because they could produce the crops they needed to sell. This early divide in monetary focus would play a significant role in how the country would form, and later, how it would almost be ruined.

With their focus on more mental exercises, the Northern colonies became far more disgruntled with the laws and taxes emerging from Europe. They had the time to calculate and analyze agreements, which resulted in a much greater sense of dissatisfaction with their ties to the parent countries. The American Revolution is remembered as a blow against England by the colonies, but part of the reason for it was the war between England and France before the American Revolution. A proxy war was fought within the colonies, and those who were under the British crown viewed the French with distrust and suspicion. This proxy war ended up costing both countries. Because the British won, the French maintained only the less populated regions within the colonies (they still "owned" large swathes of the continent, which would later be purchased from Napoleon Bonaparte by Thomas Jefferson). Had this war gone differently, it is just as likely that the colonies would have turned against both the French and the British. Either way, the focus of the different regions within the country formed their respective perspectives on slavery. The North progressively became more upset with the taxation without representation. The South was more focused on trade and their crops. By the time of the Revolution, the Southern colonies were far less enthusiastic about breaking away from the crown. They had to be persuaded it was in their best interest.

As the North worked to persuade the South of the benefits of a revolution, they increasingly drew their own opinions on slavery. The way the Southern colonies relied on slaves reminded Northern colonists of how the crown relied on them without giving them any say in how they were governed. However, they needed the Southern colonies on their side to succeed. The northern colonies could not afford to have enemies coming from across the ocean and from the South. This meant compromising with the Southern colonies and agreeing to terms that were becoming increasingly uncomfortable to the Northern colonies. This is not to say that the Northern States viewed the slaves as equals—they simply saw a similarity between their circumstances and the plight of the slaves. With each slave rebellion, the Northern colonies became increasingly more uncomfortable with the hypocrisy. This would continue long after the United States of America was founded, and it led to the Northerners assisting runaway slaves.

Chapter 2 – African Americans' Contribution to Literature, Art, and Music

There have been many African Americans recorded in the annals of American history for numerous reasons. However, the majority of those who are remembered today from the days of slavery are remembered for their roles in fighting oppression, slavery, and the hypocrisy of a system that often did not view them as people. While it is important to know these historical figures because of what they did, it means other areas have often been ignored. Though not recognized today, the African Americans who contributed to the arts played an equally vital role in the formation of the opinions of both slaves and freemen.

It should also be noted women are the predominant effort behind the arts, although some took far longer to gain the recognition they deserved. This is because they had to not only overcome the racism that was prevalent in both the North and South, but they also had to fight the sexism that refused to acknowledge their skills. Women were more likely to be educated because they tended to work inside the home more often. Men were more valuable in the fields. It was also easier to control women, so they were more accepted in the homes of their owners. The most notable exception to this pattern of disregard, William Wells Brown, is offered last in this chapter. It is clear why he was able to achieve such astonishing success even though he was largely ignored and considered a financial drain to his owner during his early years.

Limitations and Stretching Beyond Them

Slaves were very rarely educated, which meant they had few ways to record their stories. Since they did not have much time to themselves, they were unable to create much art on their own. Like early humans, slaves kept records through storytelling and singing, although many plantation owners tried to limit even these types of activities for fear the slaves were plotting.

Occasionally, slaves were taught to read and write, although the Southern colonies began to pass legislation against such slave education in 1749. A few places justified teaching slaves as long as it was in the context of Christian teachings. Still, slaves found other ways to learn, largely through self-teaching. Those who worked in homes had access to what they needed to help them learn. They would, in turn, teach other slaves what they knew.

Freemen in the Northern territories were not forbidden from learning, but few people of European descent had an active interest in assisting them. Though Africans and those of African descent were seen as human, the Northerners still did not believe they were equals. This meant that African descendants in the North had only a slightly greater likelihood of being able to learn to read and write, which set them at a severe disadvantage because they had to manage their own affairs. Financial hardship was one of the largest challenges for illiterate people, including the vast majority of those of African descent.

The exception to this was again in Pennsylvania. The Quakers actively sought to ensure everyone had the knowledge and skills necessary to survive, which meant teaching everyone to read and write. Before the Revolutionary War began, they actively worked to educate African descendants. The Quakers' work continued long after the war as well, and those who learned from them would, in turn, teach others.

By 1860, fewer than 8% of all people of African descent in the United States were literate. This severely limited not only their ability to earn and manage money, but it hampered the creation of African American art in the period leading up to the Civil War. There were a few slaves and freemen who left their cultural mark, and ironically, it was largely through writing. They were also very adept at recreating stories through their songs.

Slave Songs

From the oppression they experienced, slaves created songs as a way to chronicle their lives when there was no one to record those memories. The slave songs fit into their own genre of music and dance that tells the story of what it was like to be a slave in the Americas. Both Brazil and the United States have rich tapestries of slave songs that provide insight into the daily life and struggles of slaves, as well as their experiences of imprisonment and travel to their final destination of enslavement.

The songs served to do more than telling tales. They were also used as a way of connecting lives and resisting the inhumane treatment that slaves often endured. Even under the kindest slave owners, slaves were denied their humanity. The slave songs echoed the ill-treatment and difficulties that were nearly universal, whether a slave worked in the fields, in a home, or for business. "There is a Balm in Gilead" is one of the few examples of a known slave song that was popular prior to the Underground Railroad. It was considered a way of helping absolve sinners, and so was a spiritual healing song.

This was one of the first, and arguably the most instrumental, musical contributions from African Americans in the United States.

The slave songs provided a look into the institution that split the nation into North and South, as well as being one of the primary drivers to the American Civil War. They present the life of the slaves and the way it was instead of the way it was portrayed by slaveholders and abolitionists. Both parties focused on a few aspects of the experience without ever fully understanding what slavery was actually like. With so many slaves being illiterate, the slave songs offered a way of being creative and documenting their lives. Much like oral traditions within Europe, slave songs kept the memories of the deceased alive and brought hope in the darkness of slavery.

Lucy Terry Prince

Lucy Terry bears the distinction of being the first African American author and poet. Although she was born a slave, her poems focused on various areas of life. Born in Africa, she was sent across the Atlantic to Rhode Island. At five years old, she was purchased in Massachusetts by Captain Ebenezer Wells. In 1746, she wrote the only poem that still survives today, "Bars Fight." The poem focuses on an indigenous ambush on two families. She detailed the lives that were taken during that fight, and the one person stolen away.

While none of her other writings survived, Lucy Terry continued to live a very interesting and remarkable life. She was freed from slavery when Abijah Prince, a freeman, purchased, freed, and then married her. They wed in 1756 and had six children. Over the years, the North repeatedly proved that it did not see African descendants as equals as they constantly tried to steal land and other property from the Prince family. If not for Lucy's eloquence and ability to influence minds, the family could have suffered greatly at the injustices they faced. While she was unable to persuade Williams College to accept her son as a student, Lucy successfully argued against those who tried to claim rights to her family's land and received protection when the family needed it.

Perhaps the most awe-inspiring inspiration by this poet was her ability to present a better case than two lawyers in Vermont during a trial in which a white family tried to claim some of her family's land. She succeeded, and the justice said she had presented a better case than any he had heard from any lawyer within the state. It is a huge loss that more of her works have not survived because her mastery over English was enough to win arguments against seasoned and well-respected lawyers in Vermont.

Phillis Wheatley

Abducted in West Africa, Phillis Wheatley had a similar early experience to Lucy Terry Prince. She is the first person of African American descent to have a large body of poetry and letters survive. She is often considered the first African American poet since she has more than one surviving work. Phillis was also the first known published African American poet who enjoyed a reputation that went well beyond local fame.

Named after the slave ship that brought her to the United States and the name of the family who purchased her, Phillis began her new life in the colonies around 1761 in Massachusetts. The man who bought her, John Wheatley, was a tailor. She was meant to be a personal servant for Susanna, his wife, but her talents were very obvious to the couple. They taught her to read and write, leading her to master the English language in less than two years. She then turned her focus to Latin and Greek. By her teenage years, her writing started to reflect that of her inspiration, Alexander Pope, and her primary topics were religious in nature, particularly morality and freedom. Though not her first work, her most widely received early work was "An Elegiac Poem, on the Death of the Celebrated … George Whitefield." Her first book was called *Poems on Various Subjects, Religious and Moral*.

She married a freeman, John Peters, in 1778. She did not write much following her marriage. Unlike Lucy Terry Prince, the end of Phillis Wheatley's life was tragic. She became a servant and died poor. Several posthumous works were published, and today her letters and original copies are auctioned off for more money than the works of any other African American poet.

Harriet Powers

Though few visual works of art by those of African descent before the Civil War have survived, quilts were a visual art form that the slaves learned how to use to their advantage. Few are as well recognized for their abilities in this art form as Harriet Powers.

She was born a slave in Athens, Georgia. Not much is known about her early life, but the recognition for her quilting was documented when Jennie Smith, herself an artist, saw a particularly interesting quilt made by Harriet and asked to buy it. Though she initially refused the sale, the two stayed in touch. Roughly five years later, Harriet fell on difficult times and agreed to the sale of the quilt for $5, a significant sum around the 1880s and 1890s. The sale included a description of each of the panels in her quilt, something that Jennie Smith recorded and which is still available with the quilt today.

A second quilt was seen around 1895 on display in Atlanta during the Cotton States Exhibition. It was purchased and given to Reverend Charles Cuthbert Hall, who lived in New York.

Though she clearly made other such works of art, these are the only two surviving quilts. Even today, they are impressive for the detail and thought that went into each panel. One is a Biblical work of art that can be clearly understood by those who are familiar with the Bible (as many were at the time).

It is rather astounding how much she was able to do with so little. Living in the South, she was able to create elegant and intricate works from cloth and needle. She married after the close of the Civil War, and it was then her work was noticed because she could earn a living. She learned her skills while she was a slave, but transformed her skills into something moving for all to enjoy.

Frances Harper

Another master of the English language, Frances Harper, was born in Baltimore in 1825. Born free, she was fortunate to have an uncle who taught other free children. She began working at thirteen years old but did not stop with her education. In 1845, her first work was published, an elegant collection of prose and poetry called *Forest Leaves*.

Later, she would take her ability to shape thoughts and ideas using words and turn them into speeches and lectures, focusing on the issue of anti-slavery. Following the end of the Civil War, she went to the South to lecture and tour, as well as write. Her works are many and varied, ranging from the topics of anti-slavery to everyday life. They have earned her an interesting and permanent place in American literature.

Harriet E. Wilson

The first African American novelist was also a woman. Little is known about her life, except what can be taken as fact from her novel, *Our Nig; Sketches from the Life of a Free Black*. While much of the North decried the cruelty of slavery, the free African Americans who lived among them did not overlook their hypocrisy. The book was considered a very thinly veiled work of an autobiographical nature. The protagonist is abandoned as a young woman and is forced to work as an indentured servant. The family she worked for treated her poorly, resulting in health problems over the remainder of her life.

The book was written as a way of helping her son whom she had placed in a foster home so he could be raised under better circumstances. Unfortunately, her attempt to find a sponsor was unsuccessful and her son died less than six months after she attempted to gain a patron. The cruel treatment of a free African American highlighted just how little Northern States were willing to help those whom they claimed to want to aid. It depicts a truth that most Northerners did not want to face—they were against slavery, but they were not for equal treatment. Her work proved that life outside of slavery was not the freedom the North asserted it was. Without equality, free African Americans found themselves in a different kind of slavery disguised as servitude.

William Wells Brown

Thought to be the first African American novelist until the 1980s, William Wells Brown began life as the son of a plantation owner and slave. He was a slave, and was moved around for the first 20 years of his life. He escaped slavery in 1834, and was aided by a Quaker, Wells Brown, whose name he adopted after he was free. Wells Brown helped William reach Canada, where American laws could not force him back into slavery. Later he would move to Buffalo, New York, and work as one of the conductors on the Underground Railroad.

In the 1840s, he moved to Boston and began to write. His first major work was *Narrative of William W. Brown, a Fugitive Slave. Written by Himself.* Until Frances Harper's book was rediscovered in the 1980s, his work stood as the first novel by an African American. It was far more uplifting as well. He traveled the world talking about his experiences and lecturing.

Thomas "Blind Tom" Wiggins

One of the most phenomenal of the African American artists was born with several disadvantages beyond his race. This historical figure is virtually unknown today, despite the amazing abilities of the man. Born on May 25, 1849, Thomas Wiggins was blind and autistic. The blindness was clearly documented because it prevented him from being a productive slave. Autism, however, was not recognized because no one even realized that such a mental disorder existed. Based on the records and information on his life, though, it is considered probable, given his amazing abilities, that Thomas was autistic. It was this disability that made him into the memorable and highly respected musician that he came to be later in life.

As a slave on a plantation in Columbus, Georgia, his blindness made him considerably less useful than other slaves. Given his obvious disability, the plantation owners sold his parents, and their three children went with them. Initially, the new master, James Neil Bethune, considered killing the blind baby because he did not believe that Thomas offered any value, which meant he would cost money without making the owner anything in return. Bethune decided not to kill him, so as a child, Thomas was left to do whatever he wanted since he could not work. It was that early exploration that led to him finding the one thing that would prove he could do so much more than anyone had expected. James Bethune was an editor and a lawyer in Columbus, Georgia. This meant that the place that Thomas explored contained many extravagant things to entertain guests, including musical instruments. As a child, Tom exhibited an absolute fascination with music, and his desire to reproduce the sounds that he heard started when he was very young. Given his untrained talent, it was clear that Tom offered something completely unexpected—elegant entertainment. Having found that the child was capable of more than just roaming, Bethune now had a way to turn the child's talents into something valuable.

By the time he was eight years old, Tom had made his debut in Atlanta, Georgia. His abilities were so remarkable that Bethune hired him out as a musician for $15,000 a year. At the age of ten, Tom was the first African American to be allowed to play at the White House.

His talents went beyond reproducing existing songs. Tom began to write music of his own, and the first two pieces were published in 1860. His talents were turned to helping fund the Confederates during the Civil War. The music he composed was based on the stories he heard and the images those stories inspired. The most famous of his pieces from that time was called, "Battle of Manassas." Following the end of the Civil War, he continued as an indentured servant for Bethune, and his repertoire was still growing.

It was also discovered that his amazing hearing went beyond his ability to reproduce music—Tom could memorize poems written in other languages and recite them. Bethune took his talented "servant" to Europe where Tom played for several renowned celebrities, such as Charles Halle and Ignaz Moscheles. By 1868, Bethune was making approximately $50,000 a year for Tom's performances.

Tom's last performance was in 1905. He would die three years later, in 1908, at the home of his manager.

Chapter 3 – Independence, Slavery, Abolition, and the Compromise

When the colonists decided to revolt against the British and declared their independence, it was not a decision that was reached lightly. There were at least as many issues between the Northern and Southern colonies as there were problems between the colonies and England. The South had far more reasons to remain part of the crown than they had to leave. The Northern colonies had been progressively vocal abolitionists, which caused understandable hesitation on the part of the Southern colonies. However, the New England colonies knew that the probability of victory would significantly decrease if the Southern colonies would not join them in the struggle. Compromising their stated beliefs against slavery, they opted to ensure that slavery would be built into the new country's doctrines.

This compromise would prove to be an increasingly contentious problem between the two regions, resulting in a Civil War less than one hundred years after the founding of the new country. Between the American Revolution and the Civil War, tensions would continue to grow between the two areas of the country.

Florida – Land of the Free

While the war for American independence caused a temporary willingness of the North to ignore slavery, the Southern colonies' Southern neighbor was less willing to ignore the problem. This was in large part because it did not belong to the British.

Even before the colonies revolted against the crown, and while the Quakers fought slavery, there was a surprising location where escaped slaves could go to be free—Florida. While Florida was still a part of Spain, slaves were seen differently than they were by the British. The biggest difference was the Spanish saw slaves as unfortunate people who lost a battle or war, not as property. As such, the Spanish did not have the same view of escaped slaves from British colonies. Any slave who successfully reached Florida was considered free. This was largely because the Spanish still followed the rules or laws of the Roman Empire. Anyone they imprisoned was simply unfortunate, and they tended to take natives as slaves, just as the Romans did. If escaped slaves were willing to become Catholic and serve in the Spanish military, Spain recognized their freedom.

The Seminoles took a similar view towards escaped slaves. Having been enslaved by the Spanish, the Seminole tribes welcomed escaped slaves and offered to help them adapt to the somewhat difficult environment of Florida. Though the Seminoles and Spanish did not like each other (the Spanish treated their slaves, many of whom were Seminoles, very poorly, often resulting in their death), both viewed escaped slaves from the British colonies in the same way.

One of the largest establishments of escaped slaves was in Fort Mose, near St. Augustine. Here former slaves created a militia to fight against the English. They also fought against slave raiders who attempted to take them and other former slaves.

The Fight for Independence

The American Revolution is remembered for the colonists' desire to govern themselves and to gain their independence from a country they felt was taking from them without returning anything of significance. England felt that following the war that France was fighting within the colonies, it was only fair that taxes be raised to pay for the war. These were not the only two sides to the battle. Having lost to the British, backing the colonies was the perfect way for the French to get revenge on the British.

Outside of these highly political motives, there was a much more personal and moving reason for some of the fighters. Many of the slaves and freemen saw the potential for independence as a way of earning their freedom. After two hundred years of slavery and the active advocacy from the Northern colonies for the abolishment of slavery, it appeared that the time had arrived. Between 1773 and 1774, slaves who lived in Massachusetts drafted and submitted a petition for freedom to the colonial authorities who might heed the call as an extension of their own desires. Their dedication to the formation of a new country caused many in the Northern colonies to begin to speak out against slavery in a more vocal and forceful way, even as the colonies tried to find a solution that would benefit both regions.

Crispus Attucks
When the war finally began, it was an African American who was the first to die for the cause—Crispus Attucks. He was the first victim in the Boston Massacre of 1770.

A runaway slave who chose to live in Boston, where it was believed that African Americans would be free and treated as equals after the war, he showed his dedication to the cause. It is said that he instigated the actions that led to the killings.

His name and person were besmirched after his death by John Adams who served as the lawyer for the soldiers who shot at the colonists. The future President would use his race as an issue, claiming that Attucks exhibited "mad behavior" and "whose very look was enough to terrify any person."

It was Attucks' early experiences that caused him to believe so strongly in need for independence. Having spent much of his time as a runaway slave working on ships, he had encountered many British ships that made him feel that they were more of a threat than a benefit. The British troops stationed at the harbors were also able to offer their services for cheaper rates since they considered their help as a secondary job. The British proved to be a threat to his livelihood without offering any kind of benefit.

Despite the way Attucks was portrayed by Adams, he came to be known as a true patriot among the abolitionists. This caused other issues in the Northern areas as many of European descent still believed that he was more of a troublemaker than a patriot. Today, he is remembered as "the first to defy, the first to die," and his actions have come to be considered one of the catalysts that finally earned the United States its freedom.

Fighting for the British
Although there were some soldiers among the colonial armies of African descent who hoped for freedom after the Revolutionary War, a greater number were persuaded by the British to join them. They were told that by siding with the British, they would be granted land and self-governance on that land.

The proclamation that slaves would be freed was a trick to swell the British numbers. It did not apply to any slaves owned by someone who was loyal to the English. While slaves were told that England had banned slavery, this was also untrue. The only change for slaves in England at the time of the American Revolution was that they could not be sold outside of the country.

Most slaveholders did not promise freedom to their slaves, but that also meant they were not lying to their slaves. In fact, African descendants who stayed in Northern territories were far more likely to gain freedom than those who sided with the British. African descendants who sided with the British also left with them, but to their disappointment, the promises were almost never fulfilled. Instead of granting the former slaves what was promised, the British moved them to other lands (Sierra Leone, England, Canada, and Australia), but very little else changed.

The greatest promise of freedom came from the new Northern States.

Despite the increasing discomfort with slavery among a growing number of people within the new country, the institution was still part of life and important to the economics of the new country. Even men like Thomas Jefferson spoke about how immoral it was, yet he himself continued to own slaves until he died. He called the institution a "hideous blot" and believed it would be a significant problem for the U.S., if not the cause for its fall. Still, all this documentation for the new country was full of compromises that ensured the perpetuation of the institution of slavery. He firmly believed African Americans were mentally inferior to people of European descent, and he also believed that African Americans would never overcome their resentment towards white people. He advocated returning African Americans to a continent that many of them had never been to as a solution to prevent the country from tearing itself apart. This was in large part because he saw the two races as being two separate nations.

The Civil War proved he was partly right, but it did not create the race war he expected. Nor were the African American people as mentally incapable as he believed. By building slavery into the foundation, he ensured that there would be more tension, not less, between the two races.

Because the Northern States had a denser population of people of European descent than the Southern States, the Northern States felt that this meant they would have a much greater say in the development of the country. The compromise was made in the American Constitution that slave owners would be given an additional vote for every three out of five slaves they held. This was an incredibly reprehensible solution as it both acknowledged the humanity of the slaves and removed their right to speak for themselves, giving their voice instead to their slaveholders.

Other language was built into the Constitution ensured the perpetuation of slavery, but nothing was quite as abhorrent and hypocritical as using slaves to gain a larger voice to more easily silence the slaves.

Strong Words, Tepid Actions

Decrying slavery as being unchristian, the Northern States would either enact laws to phase out slavery or to outright ban slavery. For most of the States, the phasing out would be done through former slaves acting as indentured servants for a set amount of time or until a specific age. This was done under the assumption it would help former slaves become better at managing their own affairs. What it failed to consider was that most former slave owners did very little to help their former slaves adapt. Former slaves were treated just as poorly as before, they largely went uneducated (except in areas where there were Quakers), and the payment of wages during this time was not always honored. This caused a growing animosity between the two races throughout much of the States as those of European descent repeatedly proved that they disagreed with the idea that humans could be owned, but did not agree on equality between the races.

All the New England States had abolished slavery by 1804, but that did not mean African Americans were viewed as equals. Slavery was illegal, but so was the African American right to vote. They had curfews not given to white men, and could not travel freely. Perhaps one of the strangest laws was they were banned from serving in the military of most States by the 1830s, despite the fact so many had fought and died to help establish the new country.

As late as 1850, there were some African Americans who were still slaves in all States but Pennsylvania. They were not freed until their "servitude" ended on their twenty-eighth birthday.

Breaking Down of the Compromise

Still, the Northern States used this as a means of gaining the moral high ground against Southern States that were clearly unwilling to even consider such a move. They had rallies and strove to force the South to become as enlightened and liberated as they seemed to believe Northern States were. Ignoring their own racism and subjugation, the North increasingly saw the South as being lesser for having no plan to abolish the institution of slavery.

Several events between the American Revolution and the American Civil War caused the breakdown in the nation's ability to negotiate around the institution.

Cotton Gin
Slavery was already considered to be an integral part of the Southern lifestyle prior to 1793, but the growing movement of abolitionists in the North made it seem like eliminating slavery was inevitable.

Cotton was becoming an increasingly important crop, but it was not yet among the top three exports. This was in large part because removing seeds from cotton was an incredibly laborious process that took a substantial amount of time. It was easier to grow other products, such as tobacco, because more could be grown at a single time. Several potential solutions were provided, but none of them offered the kind of time-saving benefits that made cotton more appealing.

Then, in 1793, Eli Whitney provided a solution that not only significantly reduced the amount of time it took to remove seeds, but it also increased the Southern need for slaves. The machines were dangerous. With this new method of producing cotton, it soon became a much more important crop to the Southern States. This gave them more reason to resist the growing abolitionist movement because all parts of the young country benefited from the invention. With the increase in cotton production, New England had more raw resources to increase manufacturing. Given the struggles the Northern States had in establishing trade, this meant they had more products to offer potential clients, so they were, again, willing to compromise their beliefs for an opportunity to improve their financial stability. As uncomfortable as they were with slavery, the Northern States remained willing to negotiate for their own security. However, they did begin to make demands of their own.

Banning of Further Slave Shipments

In 1807, Congress enacted one of the first laws that began to reflect the Northern desire to get rid of slavery. At a time when the Southern States discovered they needed more slaves to produce the levels of cotton made possible by the cotton gin, Congress passed an act that forbade any further shipments of slaves from Africa, effective on January 1, 1808. This move was accomplished because some Southern representatives sided with the Northern States, although the motives were entirely different.

While the act abolished slaves from being brought to the country, it did not forbid the sale of slaves already in the country, including children. This meant that some slave owners could gain a larger market by selling their own slaves since they would have less competition. With an already large slave population (African Americans significantly outnumbered the white population), they could sustain the slave trade internally.

Chapter 4 – Fugitive Laws and One Hundred Years of Rebellion

There were many laws on the books that made neither the North nor the South happy. Northern States were not happy to aid slaveholders. When slaves escaped their captivity and reached Northern areas, the Northern States wanted to allow them to be free. However, to Southern States, this appeared to be stealing, and they thought that Northern States were going to benefit from being belligerent.

Many things great and small contributed to the growing tensions around slavery, but the frequency of slave rebellions was a cause of great concern for the South. The South wanted greater guarantees that slaves would be returned to their owners and that rebellions would be put down with greater force. Just as the European colonists were vastly outnumbered by the slaves in what later became Haiti, the Southern States had a much greater population of slaves than white people. This contributed to the fear and suspicion between the North and the South. As the North expressed greater interest in abolishing slavery and aiding escaped slaves, the South feared that slaves would rise up and kill them because they now felt they had backing from the North.

Fugitive Slave Laws

Early in America's history, the Southern States became worried and demanded reassurances that their "property" would be returned if a slave escaped to the free States in the North. With the outspoken abolitionists in the North, it seemed certain that without legal action, slaves would become free if they made it to the North.

While the North's discomfort was understandable, the fact they had been willing to compromise created an expectation and responsibility to assist in maintaining the very institution they claimed to loath. As a result, the *Fugitive Slave Act of 1793* was enacted. It ensured the Constitution, Article IV; Section 2 would be federally enforceable. This meant judges at the federal district, or circuit court would be allowed to pass final judgment on the status of anyone who was an alleged fugitive slave.

This law outraged the North. They felt it infringed on their right as States to act according to their beliefs. Because of this federal law, numerous personal-liberty laws were passed at state levels in an attempt to block federal enforcement of the law. On an individual level, people became more likely to participate in the growing movement of the Underground Railroad.

Seeing the obvious opposition and flaunting of Northern States against the law of 1793, the South demanded further legislation to ensure that the laws were executed as written. The result was the *Fugitive Slave Act of 1850*. Any alleged slave was not allowed to speak on his or her own behalf in front of the judge, nor were they allowed to have a trial by jury. Any federal marshal who refused to assist in capturing a runaway slave would be subject to heavy penalties under the law. Any individual who assisted in an escape would face stiff penalties, as well. Unsurprisingly, this led to numerous offenses of the law and caused greater grievances on both sides. The North took the law as an affront to their beliefs, and a larger number of individuals joined to assist the movement of slaves along the Underground Railroad. Northern States also passed a greater number of personal-liberty laws to further erode the law passed in 1850.

In response, Southern States began to threaten to leave the Union. There were laws passed, which were more detrimental to the South, but the States still enforced them. The North's unwillingness to cooperate with the laws that went through the proper legislative process was seen as a breach of the founders' agreements that led to the creation of the United States. While it was clearly an immoral institution, the blatant dismissal of the law by the North showed how unwilling they were to comply with agreements passed through legislative means. The South increasingly felt that the North ignored their rights and needs. It also caused a breakdown in trust, so that nothing that Abraham Lincoln could do would be seen as trustworthy. Because it had been proven that the federal government could not enforce its own laws, the Union was no longer seen as a benefit to the South.

1800 Gabriel Prosser Revolt

One of the earliest rebellions occurred in the first 25 years of the founding of the nation. Though it was unsuccessful, it caused a lot of anxiety and cracking down on slaves once the revolt was put down.

The main leader of the revolt was Gabriel Prosser. Born a slave in 1775, little else is known about the early and formative years of his life. What is known is that he had two brothers and a wife who joined in the rebellion. Gabriel was a tall (6 foot 2 inches) blacksmith, and his appearance was intimidating and awe-inspiring to other slaves. He was also known to have a good mind that made him stand out among the slaves.

Gabriel's plan appeared to mirror the Haitian Revolution, a revolution that resulted in the near complete annihilation of all white people on the island. Gabriel planned to kill all white people in the city of Richmond. He would make an exception for those who had historically assisted slaves, including Quakers, Methodists, and French people (which was highly ironic considering the French residents had been the victims of the Haitian Revolution). Gabriel saw his future as being the monarch of the new domain, and all slaves would be freed.

Striving to create units that could act as the units of the other recent revolutions (American, French, and Haitian), Gabriel would create a large following, estimated to be in the thousands.

The plan ultimately failed because two slaves felt some loyalty, or at least sympathy for, their masters, and told the Virginia authorities about the plot. Gabriel realized the plan had been compromised before the attack that had been scheduled for August 30th. He and his followers dispersed as Richmond increased its protection. Initially, Gabriel escaped to Norfolk, but he was again betrayed. Other slaves who wanted the reward for turning him into the authorities. He was tried on the 25th of September and executed on the 26th of September in 1800.

Instead of gaining their freedom, slaves were more violently repressed because of the plot. The relaxing of the system and better treatment of slaves led the Southern States to believe the rebellion was proof it only encouraged greater resistance to slavery. It was also seen as proof that slaves should not be taught to read and write because it had led to Gabriel understanding what happened in the world at large.

1822 – Denmark Vesey Revolt

Less than 25 years after the unsuccessful Gabriel Prosser Revolt, the largest rebellion in U.S. history occurred in Charleston, South Carolina. Telemaque arrived in the city in 1783 as a slave of a ship's captain. He bought himself from Captain Joseph Vesey. Now a free man, Telemaque took the name of his former master and built up an amazing reputation for his skill and dedication to his craft as a carpenter.

In 1818, Vesey became a part of the African Methodist Episcopal congregation in Charleston. As a slave center, the church was a threat, and it was temporarily closed that same year. This was viewed as an affront to their religion, and many of the parishioners became determined to ensure they had a place to freely worship. It was also a very likely motivator for the revolt.

Now in his 50s, Vesey planned a rebellion that would take the slaves from Charleston to the free country of Haiti. His plan was four years in the making and was not meant to result in the slaughter of everyone. Instead, the plan was to help as many slaves escape to Haiti as quickly as possible after strategically killing those who might stop their flight.

The plan called for slaves to awaken and depart at midnight on July 14th; the day celebrated as Bastille Day in France. They would kill their masters, ensuring they could make it without alarms being raised. Though Vesey knew where a large stock of guns was stored, slaves were largely untrained in how to use the weapons. Instead of taking the guns, he encouraged slaves to use what they had on hand and already knew how to use.

He had also learned a lesson from the failed Gabriel Prosser rebellion, and he ensured those who were brought into the plan could be trusted.

However, history repeated itself when two slaves notified their owners of the plan in June. A major was notified and brought the militia in to take Vesey and his wife into custody. They were both hanged on July 2nd, just 12 days before the revolt was supposed to liberate throngs of slaves. It also resulted in the complete destruction of his church and a complete lockdown on the city. Charleston patrolled the ports to ensure slaves did not learn of any activity outside of the country since events in Haiti had clearly influenced the once well-respected Vesey.

1831 – Nat Turner

Unlike the previous rebellions that were defeated before they could even be enacted, Nat Turner's rebellion was the only rebellion that saw any degree of success.

Like Gabriel, Nat Turner lived in Virginia, and his rebellion would begin in Southampton County. In his early life, Nat Turner was a slave of Benjamin Turner, who wanted the child to be taught to read and write along with heavy religious instruction. He was sold several times, becoming more vocal about his religion and a greatly respected preacher among the slaves. During the 1820s, he began to speak as if he were a new Moses meant to bring his people out of bondage. Unlike the other leaders, Nat heard voices and believed in his greatness and divine purpose.

He did not have a grand plan, nor did he have the numbers amassed by the other two rebels. This turned out to be the reason for the initial success of his revolution. With the help of 75 slaves, the somewhat impromptu rebellion began, resulting in the death of 51 white people.

Nat Turner successfully hid for six weeks following the rebellion. The Southern States experienced a heightened fear of what would happen over this time because there had never been such a successful slave rebellion in the country's history. However, Turner's luck ended after those six weeks and he, along with 16 others, were found, tried, and killed. Their actions resulted in further restrictions and cruelty in the name of self-defense by slave owners.

There was also an intense interest in how Turner succeeded where others had not. While he was alive and being held in Jerusalem, Virginia (where he was hung), a lawyer named Thomas R. Gray spent time talking to Turner about his actions. Their conversations were published nearly verbatim (as closely as possible, according to Gray), offering an insightful look into the mind of the man. The stories Turner told began when he was young and progressed over the course of his life. It is this narrative of his life that has been taken as fact and resulted in a full movie of the events attributed to the discussions between the prisoner and the attorney.

1839 – Amistad

Slave rebellions were not confined to the land as the events of the Amistad proved in 1839. This was the only truly successful rebellion, and it occurred on a Spanish cargo ship that was carrying slaves. The Amistad was scheduled to arrive in New York in August of 1839.

The 53 Africans onboard, who were to be sold into slavery in Cuba, overthrew the Spanish. The Africans attempted to force the Spanish to return them to Africa. The British invoked the Treaty of Ghent, which prohibited the new enslavement of Africans, forcing the US to get involved in the case. The US helped to capture the ship for the Spanish because of Pinckney's Treat, which established a friendly relationship between the two countries and defined the border between Florida and the US. Though the US helped the Spanish retake the ship, they worked toward ensuring the African passenger's freedom because of the Treaty of Ghent. The Amistad was docked in Connecticut. By landing in Connecticut, a state that had abolished slavery, the men were considered free.

It resulted in one of the earliest showdowns between the judiciary and executive branches. President Van Buren was willing to acknowledge the Spanish claim and have the ship continue South to Cuba where the captured Africans would be enslaved and punished for the mutiny. The Secretary of State said that the President did not have this authority and that the judiciary branch had already ruled the Spanish were in violation by bringing free Africans over to enslave them. Based on this state ruling, the free Africans could not be released to the Spanish.

The decision was ultimately taken to the Supreme Court where the status of the Africans was debated. Either they were the property of Spain, which meant they needed to follow the Treaty of 1795, or they were free Africans who were illegally abducted by the Spanish. Former President John Quincy Adams argued the men were free. His argument was made by a panel of judges who were more inclined to side with the South, so he had to prove the issue wasn't with slaves, but the abduction and illegal enslavement of free men. The argument focused on the fact that the Africans were never Spanish citizens but free persons, and the act was illegal. The court sided with Adams and Spain was told that, while the treaty still held, it was not meant to be extended to the enslavement of free people as that infringed on the rights of Africans.

The men were returned to their homes in Africa, and the Spanish continued to demand compensation for damages after the case was settled.

1856 – John Brown

John Brown was a white man raised in the North in a family that was staunchly against slavery. Though his personal life was troubled, largely because of his unsuccessful business dealings, he worked as a conductor on the Underground Railroad and was devoted to the cause.

When he was 55 years old, he moved to the Kansas Territory to try to find financial stability. Kansas was a hotly contested area between the North and the South. The North did not want any new areas to have slaves, and the South wanted to extend the territories where slavery was allowed.

Following an attack in Lawrence, Kansas in May 1856, John Brown organized a small group of men and went to the homes of men believed to be staunch slavery proponents. Brown then had the men dragged from their homes and killed. After this initial success, Brown and his followers went into Missouri and freed eleven more slaves after killing their owners.

He then returned to New England to get funding to try a similar tactic in the South. Brown trained 21 men to help him. They planned to attack Harpers Ferry, Virginia after freeing all slaves. They would then break into and steal the weapons and ammunition in the arsenal there in an attempt to encourage an armed revolt. This proved to be a serious flaw in the plan because the slaves did not join them. The Marines responded to the threat, and under the leadership of Robert E. Lee, John Brown and his followers were killed or captured.

Though the North thought of him as a hero and the South considered him a villain, people on both sides disagreed with his violent methods. Following his trial, which was much longer and thorough than the trials of any of the slaves (save those on the Amistad who were found to be freemen), Brown was sentenced to death. At the beginning of December 1859, he was hanged.

He gave the jailer a message before he was led to his execution. "… the crimes of this guilty, land: will never be purged away, but with Blood. I had as I now think: vainly flattered myself that without very much bloodshed; it might be done." This proved to be very prophetic as the Civil War began with the secession of South Carolina in 1860.

Chapter 5 – The Beginning of the End of Slavery

The laws of the new country began to reflect the values of the two different perspectives of abolitionists and slaveholders. Perhaps, it may have taken longer to come to a head had the country not exponentially grown due to the Louisiana Purchase. This purchase was meant to increase the size of the country but quickly showed just how divided the nation was on several issues. Slavery was easily the most divisive of the problems these new territories faced.

Slavery was always a contentious issue, but by the middle of the nineteenth century, the U.S. was too divided on the issue to continue as it had in the past. With tensions high and both sides unwilling to listen to the other, the middle decades of the nineteenth century would prove to be the tipping point for slavery.

Between 1820 and the beginning of the Civil War, there were many events and people who played critical roles in forcing the nation to finally decide how to handle the institution.

1820 – Missouri Compromise

As the U.S. expanded west, the nation was faced with the challenge of trying to keep both the interests of the North and the South equal. This meant allowing the spread of slavery into some territories and banning slaves in others. Missouri was in the South, so it was a slave state. The new state of Maine was in the North, so it became a free state. Called the Missouri Compromise, it set up more than just the status of the two new States in the Union—it stated that slavery would not be allowed in any of the territories that were above a specific line of latitude.

The problem stemmed from the request that Missouri submitted to be allowed into the Union as a slave state. At the time, the country was evenly divided between slave and free States, and the addition of one slave state was thought to tip this delicate balance. The debates and arguments lasted for much of 1819. It was only in 1820 that the debate was finally settled so that Maine, which was once part of Massachusetts, would be added at the same time.

Predictably, the verdict upset both sides. The South felt it was an overreach on the part of Congress to dictate laws about slavery. The North was angry that Congress was continuing to compromise with the South over something they did not want to spread further.

1846 – Wilmot Proviso

By 1846, abolitionists did not feel that the Missouri Compromise went far enough to ensure the country did not allow the spread of slavery. David Wilmot sponsored the proposal and started a debate that would help to finally pull the country apart. Ultimately, the Wilmot Proviso created the Republican Party—a party that was strongly opposed to slavery.

The Wilmot Proviso was written following the end of the Mexican War (1845 to 1846). The US wanted to annex the territories of Texas, California, and others. Wilmot represented those who did not want any more territories or States to be brought into the Union with slavery being permitted in the state. The territories that were to be taken from Mexico were ideal because slavery had been abolished in Mexico in 1829. Since slavery was not already present in these regions, the Wilmot Proviso sought to ensure the territories continued to honor the rules followed by Mexico regarding slavery.

The House passed the measure, but it never made it through the Senate, despite its several efforts. The Senate ignored the proviso every time it was added as an amendment to various bills, but it kept the problem at the forefront of the thinking during that time.

1854 – Kansas-Nebraska Act

Although neither side had been happy about the Missouri Compromise, it stood until it was repealed in 1854. The *Kansas-Nebraska Act of 1854* gave popular sovereignty to those who settled in U.S. territories. Ironically, Abraham Lincoln's opponent for the presidency, Stephen A. Douglas, proposed it. The act undid the requirement that any States above a specified line of latitude would be free States. The result was Bleeding Kansas, as both sides turned to violence. Both Kansas and Nebraska were above this line of latitude, yet they chose to include the ownership of slaves.

Neither side was willing to continue compromising, and both felt they were in the right. It was part of the reason for the rebellion started by John Brown. His violent approach helped to begin the downward spiral that convinced the North and South they would never negotiate and resolve the problem as a single country.

The President at the time, Franklin Pierce, had to act, and he sent troops to halt the violence. They were also required to end the legislature of Kansas that was against slavery because Pierce was pro-slavery. An election was held in the territory to vote for how the territory would be brought into the country. When pro-slavery won, abolitionists said it was a result of election fraud, and the election was not upheld. This meant it took longer for the territory to become a state and incensed the South. A new constitution was drawn up for the state, and it was clear that anti-slavery settlers now outnumbered the pro-slavery settlers.

As another stroke of irony, Kansas was added to the Union as a free state, but it was too late. When it was admitted, the Union had already lost eight States to secession. It had been a key factor in that decision and so was brought into a country on the verge of war.

Frederick Douglass

Easily one of the most renowned and respected African Americans in the country's history, Frederick Douglass was an elegantly outspoken opponent of slavery. Though he was an equally impressive writer, he is best known for his stance and speeches, which put into words what many in the North felt about slavery.

Considered a leader during the nineteenth century, Frederick Douglass lived a long and interesting life. Born to a slave in 1818, he was a slave until he turned 20 and escaped from his master. He took his name from the famous work by Sir Walter Scott, *The Lady of the Lake*. His love of literature turned into a desire to write, and Douglass chronicled his early life in *Narrative of the Life of Frederick Douglass, An American Slave*, which was published in 1845. There were two follow-up autobiographies in 1855 and 1881, which looked at his escape from slavery and his life over nearly seven decades.

While the books were clearly meant to be anti-slavery works, they also provided insight into the life of a slave for the majority of people in the North and people who did not own slaves in the South. The works are regarded as classic works in American literature.

As instrumental as his writings were to the African American culture, it was his endeavor to free slaves that made him a legend in his lifetime. Douglass lived a very public and open life, never hiding his opinions or masking the way he felt. One of his most eye-opening works was called "What to the Slave Is the Fourth of July?" It pointed out how the day has as much significance to the slave as to the British because the formation of the country was built on loss; for the slave, it was a loss of hope that their situation would change for the better.

His career contending for African Americans never stopped; it merely evolved over time. Once slaves were freed, the South would try to oppress them and treat them like second-class citizens under the Jim Crow laws. However, Douglass did not just point out the illegalities of the South; he was vocal about the hypocrisy and inequality practiced in the North, as well.

Douglass had a large platform for his work. As a resident of Rochester, New York, he was the editor of *The North Star*, a highly influential newspaper by African Americans. It would change names over the years (*Frederick Douglass' Paper* and *The Douglass Monthly*), but the principles and opinions remained constant over his time as the editor.

To Douglass, the Civil War was a necessity to end the evil practice of slavery. He pressed for emancipation as the war raged. During the war, he was also an advisor to Abraham Lincoln, and he is credited with having persuaded the President to finally emancipate all slaves. His views and words about the war were well regarded by both sides after the war was over because it provided a way of understanding the tragedy that was the Civil War.

Despite his loathing of slavery, Douglass loved the South because it was his first home. The war was a necessity to bring his home to the right side of history, but he very much wanted to see it prosper and grow with both races learning to coexist peacefully. He died in 1895, the same year that saw the rise of Booker T. Washington.

Harriet Beecher Stowe

Harriet Beecher Stowe was a staunch opponent of slavery, and her works of literature helped people to better understand it from a different perspective. While she was a white woman born in Connecticut in 1811, her works helped to illustrate the injustice of slavery to a much wider audience.

Her most famous work was *Uncle Tom's Cabin*, published in 1851. While it is seen as patronizing and condescending today, it showed the reality of slavery in terms that other white people could better understand.

Her work was based on her interactions with slaves, giving it some authenticity. The book aimed to convince Northerners to continue to fight against slavery by aiding escaped slaves. Clearly, the South saw it as a breach of agreements that were part of the foundation of the country.

In 1856, she wrote a follow-up book called *Dred: A Tale of the Great Dismal Swamp*, a work that examined the cruelty of the decision from the Dred Scott case. While Dred Scott was a character in the book, he was not the main character. Instead, she wrote about the people who held his life in their hands, largely white men in the South who had no incentive to see justice.

Chapter 6 – The Rallying Movements and Moments, and the Civil War

As laws and people addressed the issue of slavery, others acted on their own. The middle decades of the 1800s saw some of the most heroic and heinous actions in American history. President Abraham Lincoln also tried to reach one final compromise as States threatened to secede from the country that had been deeply divided on many issues, but one in particular—slavery.

Slavery had been a divisive issue that plagued the nation from the very beginning. It did not take one hundred years for it to reach a breaking point where the nation would either entirely abolish the institution of slavery, or it would split into different nations because of it. Numerous events finally drove the final wedge between the two ideologies. The nation had been spiraling downward towards this conclusion, but the final years leading up to the war were fraught with tension, and every little thing proved the point both sides were trying to make. Neither side would listen to the other because they were beyond compromise.

The North was never going to be the part of the country to leave the Union. The Revolutionary War was largely their idea, and they clung to the ideas that led to war with England to try to keep the country together.

It was always going to be the South that would finally make a move. As soon as one Southern state left, the rest of the pro-slavery States followed. The North could not accept the secession, and so a Civil War began and finally ended the problem that had plagued the country since its earliest days.

Harriet Tubman and the Underground Railroad

One of the greatest problems the South had with the United States of America was that many abolitionists actively sought to undermine slavery. While they did not come to the South and directly attack the institution, they did assist slaves who successfully escaped from Southern plantations and reached the North.

The biggest known coordinated effort to help escaped slaves was called the Underground Railroad. The most famous (or infamous to the South) leader of this effort was a woman named Harriet Tubman.

Founding of the Underground Railroad

Harriet Tubman did not found the Underground Railroad. It started at the beginning of the nineteenth century. It grew over the course of several decades, and by the time the Civil War broke out it had become the most successful network for freeing slaves. There are very few records from the efforts of the early days. In fact, much of what is known about the Underground Railroad was information released after the Civil War had ended. Those who coordinated the effort did not want to compromise the slaves making their way to freedom, but more importantly, they did not want to endanger the people who were willing to risk their lives to help the slaves. As the federal government passed further legislation against helping escaped slaves, the effort became an increasingly dangerous endeavor. Historians estimate that one hundred thousand slaves successfully achieved freedom between the earliest known days of the Underground Railroad in 1810 and the beginning of the Civil

War in 1860. Nearly all the slaves who made the trip through the network came from States that bordered the North. Very few slaves, if any, from the Deep South, could make their way to the Underground Railroad. They simply did not have the necessary assistance to find the people who were willing to support the network.

What is known about the highly secretive effort is that it was comprised of African Americans and Caucasians who felt slavery was morally wrong. It is unknown where the railway began, but small groups of people who were willing to risk the illegal activity on moral grounds began to connect with one another. Over time, the anti-slavery connections grew until there was a much larger, more intricate, group of people who used a free-flowing method of working around police efforts and Southern attempts at enforcing the laws. They decided to name the effort the Underground Railroad because it provided safe havens for slaves, and they were all kept secret. These locations would change, making it nearly impossible for law enforcement to predict where the safe havens would be.

There were several unique ways of passing on information. Songs were sung that gave hints at where to meet, how many slaves were making the passage, and details about their trip. Even more interesting, there was a secret language.

Most activities took place at night to more easily slip the groups through and past people who sought to capture slaves. Homes of the people helping were used as stations along the network and included places for slaves to hide if needed. Slaves were taken between the different points by a conductor. The slaves could not make it from one of these points to the next one because they were not familiar with the terrain. Only the conductor knew where they were going, making it a critical role along the way to freedom.

Harriet Tubman's Early Life and Involvement With the Underground Railroad

Many famous historical figures supported the Underground Railroad, including Frederick Douglass, Samuel Burris, William Lloyd Garrison, and Obadiah Bush. However, there was one person who not only supported it, but she was also an active member of the railroad serving in a critical role. The most famous conductor on the Underground Railroad was Harriet Tubman, an escaped slave.

Born a slave in Maryland, her original name was Araminta Ross, and she was one of 11 children. The slave owners saw her as a valuable slave who could be hired out to others to assist with tending to babies (similar to a nursemaid). The job was far riskier than it sounds. She had to stay awake through the entire night in case the child woke and began to cry. If the hired slave fell asleep, she was whipped as punishment.

From an early age, she was against the idea of slavery, and it was always her intention to escape from it and become free. When she was still young, she was ordered to help in punishing another slave. She refused. The slave she was supposed to help punish began to run. In response, the man doling out the punishment threw a heavy iron weight to try to stop him. The weight missed the escaping slave and hit Harriet Tubman. The event nearly killed her because the weight was heavy enough to crush her skull. She had a large scar on her head and seizures were a regular part of the remainder of her life.

Her name changed in 1844 when she married a freeman named John Tubman. In addition to taking his last name, she also took a new first name, her mother's name.

Five years later, Harriet feared that she and another slave would be sold. Instead of waiting, Tubman decided to escape. Her husband refused to join her, but two of her brothers decided it was worth the risk. Their only guidance was the North Star. Her brothers did not make it as they became too afraid of what would happen to them and returned to the plantation. Harriet pressed on and reached Philadelphia. Once in the North, she got a job as a servant to earn money. For Tubman, her wages weren't just to sustain herself—she always planned to use the money to help other slaves finally break free of their shackles.

Harriet Tubman was called the "Moses of her people" because of the amount of time and effort she dedicated to ensuring the freedom of as many people as she could.

The Underground Railroad was effectively over with the Emancipation Proclamation because the country no longer acknowledged slaves as property. They were people and could not be owned by anyone. This meant that those who worked on the railroad no longer had to ensure slaves made it safely to new homes—as long as they were in the North, they were free.

Though the railroad ended during the Civil War, Harriet Tubman continued her efforts to help African Americans. Working as a nurse, cook, and spy for the United States, she continued to play an important role for the country. Her work as a conductor was incredibly useful to her and the country because she was already very familiar with the land where she was needed.

Dred Scott

Another point of contention between the North and the South was the decision on a case called *Dred Scott v John F.A. Sandford*. The case reached the Supreme Court in March of 1857.

It was a controversial case because it involved a slave, Dred Scott, and his master, both of who had moved to a state that had abolished slavery. Because he lived in a state that did not allow slavery, it was argued that Dred Scott must be free. It was illegal for anyone to own a slave, so bringing a slave into the state should be considered as a way of freeing the slave.

The Supreme Court did not agree with this assessment and went much further to undermine other arguments by abolitionists.

First, they said that residing in a free state did not inherently mean a slave was free. If a slave owner did not specifically allow the slave to have his or her freedom, the slave was not free.

Second, the court ruled that African Americans were not citizens of the U.S. It was acknowledged that African Americans could be citizens of States where they could vote, but there were few who voted even in free States. It also did not make sense because if someone was a citizen of a state, he or she must also be a citizen of the country. This ruling meant that African Americans could not sue within the country. Under this assumption, the lawsuit was illegal because Dred Scott did not have the jurisdiction to make his case within the U.S.

The final part of the Supreme Court ruling was the Missouri Compromise was illegal. Most of the Court argued the compromise was unconstitutional 37 years after it had been passed. The case did not specifically look at this, but the Supreme Court used the opportunity to strike down a compromise that many of the justices did not like.

Unfortunately, the court was not even closely divided. Only two justices sided with Scott. It is often called the worst decision by the American Supreme Court in its history. The judges were largely conservative and very much pro-slavery. Their final ruling is considered judicial overreach, taking into consideration elements of the case that were not being questioned to further their own agenda. It was a self-inflicted wound that created suspicion and mistrust between the judicial branch and other areas of the government.

Because of the decision from the Dred Scott verdict, the Supreme Court has tried to keep rulings to very limited interpretations and fine-tuning of the laws.

Lincoln's Compromise

Abraham Lincoln is widely considered a liberator of slaves, but before the Civil War, he was more willing to negotiate with the South. His reputation as a liberator stemmed from the South's leaving the Union, and had the South won the war; his proclamation would have meant almost nothing.

Before the war started, it was clear to men like Lincoln the nation had finally come to the tipping point that Jefferson had warned about at the beginning of the nineteenth century. As the North and South had successfully negotiated peace, he hoped they could continue to find solutions that would not result in bloodshed.

The Kansas-Nebraska Act was the solution created by Stephen A. Douglas while he was running for President. His opponent was Abraham Lincoln. The idea behind the Kansas-Nebraska Act proved to be less than ideal, much to Douglas's surprise. Instead of unifying his party behind him, violence erupted, and the result was called Bleeding Kansas. People had reached the point where words were no longer adequate, and they turned to violence as the solution to the slavery debate.

Lincoln argued his opponent's resolution was unnecessary because the Missouri Compromise provided the necessary solution to the question of slavery in territories and new States. It was not something the people of the territory or new state should vote on as it was already decided. He argued that the Kansas-Nebraska Act not only failed to resolve the problem, but it reopened the wound about the slavery question.

Because he had fought so strongly against slavery in the territories and free States, the South was not pleased when Lincoln ultimately won the presidency. Given his stance during the campaign, they did not suspect he would enforce the laws. This put the President in a very difficult position, as he had to prove he was willing to uphold the law without upsetting the abolitionists who had elected him.

Lincoln saw the presidency as being about representation. His job was to ensure the safety and growth of the country, which meant compromising even on things he might have been morally opposed to aiding. Unfortunately, by the time he took office, the Southern States were already going through with their threat and had declared their independence from the U.S.

The South's hasty departure, in part, because Lincoln had won the election, was granted too early. Though he opposed slavery, Lincoln did not feel the President had the power to end the institution. It was something that required a much larger source of support. However, it was true that he wanted to keep slavery from spreading further as the country grew. Many Southerners felt that was enough of a difference in ideology to warrant their leaving the Union.

Despite the Southern States' dislike for the new President, there was only one state that was willing to make the decision alone—South Carolina. The other States refused to go along with the idea without having other States already stepping out of the country first. Once South Carolina left, the remaining Southern States quickly submitted their declarations of departure from the Union.

The question then became, was it possible to leave the United States peacefully? The South felt that it was their right. The North and Lincoln disagreed with them. Still Lincoln did try to keep the South talking so they would remain part of the country. Now, abolition was not even a consideration, just the spreading of slavery to other areas of the country.

Beginning of the War and the Declaration of Emancipation

Presidents had faced an increasingly difficult problem when dealing with slavery. President James Buchanan spent a considerable amount of time trying to assuage fears and get the States together to come up with a solution, a suggestion that Southern States refused to comply with.

With the Presidential election of 1860 looming, Southern States began to discuss how they would handle a Lincoln victory. The States had a solution, but South Carolina was the one that first acted on it. With that declaration, the U.S. was faced with a challenge like it had never seen before—was it possible to leave the Union after a state joined it?

Though there were other factors involved, slavery was certainly one of the primary (and most emotionally fueled) reasons for the divide. The country could no longer continue to ignore the hypocrisy that was built into a nation claiming to love freedom yet denying it for so many.

Frederick Douglass was instrumental in advising Lincoln on how to deal with the problem the South had proposed. Initially, the President was reluctant to abolish slavery because he feared it would burn a bridge with the South. By showing a willingness to negotiate, the President thought the States might rescind the idea. Many of those who advised Lincoln were against the idea, as well. Some were more pragmatic than others, such as General George McClellan. McClellan said the North needed a decisive victory so they knew they would win before forcing the issue of freedom onto States that already had enough reasons to fight them. Lincoln had decided to emancipate the slaves, but he chose to wait for a big victory before going through with it.

That victory did come. Antietam was one of the worst battles of the Civil War, and it proved to be a turning point. Only five days later, on September 22, 1862, Lincoln issued the Emancipation Proclamation. The proclamation would be effective as of January 1, 1863, unless the Southern States rejoined the Union before that time. If any of the States had returned to the US of their own volition prior to the war ending, it is very likely that slavery would have persisted much longer into American history.

This ironically gave Southerners a much greater reason to fight because they saw it as an attack on their culture. Many States that seceded did so by very slim margins, with most white, non-slaveholders voting against secession.

Texas Slaves, Post-Civil War

Texas sided with the Confederacy during the Civil War, but the state was far away from most of the front lines. This also meant that Texas was a long way for the news of the war's end to travel. It is not surprising that during the Civil War, more slaves were brought into the state since the outlook of the war was initially in the South's favor.

The slaves were very much aware that the war was occurring because so many people were involved from all over Texas. Though very few battles were fought in Texas, a large percentage of the population joined the war effort. It was impossible for the slaves to be unaware of the war, so they learned their freedom was a primary cause of the war.

When the war finally ended, it took weeks for the people of Texas to learn about the loss by the South, including the slaves. The news finally reached the state when Union soldiers landed in Galveston, Texas, to occupy and begin the reconstruction of the state. Upon his arrival, General Gordon Granger proclaimed that the war was over and that slavery was no longer allowed in the country. This meant that all the slaves were now free.

The slaves in Texas where the last slaves to be set free, and the day when General Gordon Granger declared freedom is still celebrated as Juneteenth.

However, like the citizens of many other States, Texans were upset at losing the war, and the loss of their slaves, resulting in a real change to their standard of living. They sought to ensure that the former slaves remained in poverty and dependent on their former masters through numerous means, such as the sharecropping system.

13th Amendment

Even though Abraham Lincoln had declared the slaves to be free, there were no laws to back up the proclamation. This was finally rectified by the addition of a new amendment to the Constitution. As it was the 13th amendment made to the United States Constitution, it became known as the 13th Amendment.

The amendment was proposed in January of 1865, just a few months before the end of the Civil War. Because the Southern States had already pulled all their representatives, senators, and judges out of Washington, D.C., the amendment had no real detractors when it was written. Although the amendment was not passed until the end of the year the South had been returned to the Union, the amendment faced no significant hurdles to its passing. However, this did not mean that all the States approved it. Several Southern States held out against its ratification. The last state to ratify the 13th Amendment was Mississippi in 2013, highlighting just how adverse some of the States were to being forced to accept the loss of the war and their slaves. Fortunately, ratification does not require a unanimous decision; only three-fourths of all the States need to agree for an amendment to succeed.

President Andrew Johnson from the state of Tennessee was serving as President at the time of the ratification because Abraham Lincoln had been assassinated earlier in the year.

The Corwin Amendment

As Southern States became more vocal about their desire to leave the United States, many people looked for solutions to quieten the anger and resentment that was so prevalent in the country. One of the most notable was Thomas Corwin. He was a representative from Ohio and a staunch Republican. An amendment was written while he was chairman of the Committee of 33.

The entire purpose of the committee was to create an amendment that would quell the open hostilities and talk of dividing the country. The amendment was specifically intended to stop the Southern States from going through with their threat to leave the Union, and it was written at the request of President James Buchanan. The committee included one person from each state in the Union. It was brought to the floor in January 1861, but it did not pass. Several more attempts were made, but with the election of Abraham Lincoln, all hope for an amendment was lost. Southern States decided that the time for talk was over and that it was time to act.

Conclusion

The earliest history of slaves in North America set the stage for centuries of oppression, abuse, and mistreatment of an entire population. Many of the problems in the United States of America today originated from this early treatment and abuse. The initial problem was very clear at the founding of the nation because so many already saw the inherent problem with declaring themselves freed while keeping other people in chains. However, while an increasing number of white people were uncomfortable with the hypocrisy, far fewer saw African Americans as equal.

The way they were treated, put down and oppressed caused African Americans to reflect on the most effective ways to reach the members of the populace who often failed to see them as people. From the early days, rebellions met with varying levels of success. Following the triumph of the Haitian Rebellion, slaves and freemen were forced to consider nonviolent methods of accomplishing their freedom. The methods used during the Haitian Rebellion proved to be detrimental as a military state rose from the bloody revolution. By contrast, the nonviolent arguments and the growing number of European descendants who were uncomfortable with slavery were more likely to succeed than a violent revolution. The United States had already demonstrated that it was willing to listen to arguments against slavery, but their reaction to violent slave resistance was widespread condemnation and harsher conditions for slaves.

Long before Gandhi showed how to express a group's right to be treated as equals, African Americans had found the best way to gain recognition was by using the same logic and arguments the Americans used to gain their freedom from the British. With so many people uncomfortable from the start with the idea of harboring oppression in a country that meant to be based on freedom, it was an idea that resonated. Through logic, literature, and persistence, African Americans gradually reached a circumstance where it was impossible to ignore their humanity. All of this was done as both the North and the South sought different degrees of inequality with African Americans. Some of the most influential people were not white, and their eloquence caused some to rethink the bias. Unfortunately, the huge disparity in education ensured that the white people were continually proven right in their superior thinking. Of course, this was not actual superiority as they actively sought to keep African Americans from learning. Like a cruel self-fulfilling prophecy, this way of thinking would last long after the Civil War decided the fate of slavery as an institution in the country.

Despite all of this, African Americans continued to work toward equality. Centuries of struggling helped to create some of the most renowned figures in American history, like Fredrick Douglass and Harriet Tubman. Legal cases based on biases and inherently flawed logic about the African Americans' status was gradually overturned through this persistence. The most notorious example of this blatant cruelty was in the case brought before the Supreme Court for Dred Scott. To the shame of the nation, it was hardly an isolated incident. Racism was rampant in all but a few white communities, and African Americans learned to value the friendship offered by them, particularly the Quakers.

The Civil War ended one of the darkest, most hypocritical institutions in the young country's history. Though it had long been hoped that the problem would eventually be resolved peacefully, the fact that the institution was part of the foundation of the country meant that slaveholders felt entitled to the people they purchased. It was a compromise that should not have been brokered by the North in the early days. Although it took hundreds of years to gain that recognition, slaves eventually did gain their freedom.

Throughout those hundreds of years, African Americans were contributing to the history and enriching the country through the same means as every other ethnicity. Their achievements are rarely highlighted the way the white mans are, which makes their place all the more noteworthy. With so many slaves escaping and turning their lives into something noble and self-sacrificing, it shows just how vastly different the reality was from the stereotype of the African American. Though they were denied citizenship, the contributions of African Americans helped to create a complete picture of their American experience and their ability to rise above the horrors to prove their own values and humanity. Their success was achieved largely through peaceful resistance and through logic and persuasion.

Freedom from slavery was the first decided victory for African Americans, but there was still a long way to go until they would be treated like American citizens. Their persuasion and nonviolence would later work again to fight against discrimination across the country. However, the struggles of African Americans from the time of the colonization through the end of the Civil War were the foundation by which every other success would be possible. An increasing number of African American voices started to sound throughout the country as it sought to heal the wounds of war.

Part 2: Reconstruction through the Civil Rights Movement

Introduction

The Civil War ended, and slaves were freed from their shackles, but they were not free in the same way that Caucasian Americans were. From unfair trials and denial of their basic human rights to being treated like second-class citizens, there was no sense of real equality. Even in the Northern States where slavery had been condemned, African Americans were not treated as equals. It was commonly felt they should not be slaves, but that did not mean they should have access to the same opportunities, or in the same manner, as Caucasian Americans.

The next 100 years was a slow progression of seeing African Americans as unfortunate people to be pitied for their inferiority to realizing that African Americans were just as capable when given the same resources and opportunities. The African American community learned how to band together to stand together.

Former slaves soon learned that the chances of change were slim in the South. Their former masters quickly began to implement laws and requirements that ensured the former slaves would never have the same opportunities and rights of their Caucasian counterparts. For those who were able, there was a large movement out of the oppressive South to places where the chances of equality were more hopeful. For those who remained in the South, the seeds of change were sown through strength and courage.

Art, music, and sports proved to be areas where African Americans could clearly express their pain, struggles, and hopes for the future. The Harlem Renaissance gave birth to some of the most well-known authors and artists in the U.S. The effects of this movement are still felt today. These artistic means of expression were not limited to Harlem, though. In the South, former slaves came to create some of the most inspirational and heartfelt works and musical genres – particularly Jazz.

Though it took more than 50 years, the African American community finally found its voice, and from that, the Civil Rights Movement began. Some truly courageous people stepped forward, despite the intimidation, legal ramifications, and death threats. Several notable figures spearheaded the movement, but they did not stand alone. All those who gathered at the Washington Monument in August of 1963 or marched in Selma, forced the rest of the country to begin analyzing what was considered tradition or common sense and how things should be for everyone. The U.S. was forced to question the prejudice and cruelty that had been inflicted on African Americans, even after they had been freed from slavery. It became increasingly clear that freedom from the institution of slavery meant little when racism had negated the American Dream for an entire race. The Civil Rights Movement showed that the descendants of the slaves were no more a threat than the slaves had been – they simply wanted the same opportunities and rights that Emancipation had promised them.

Chapter 6 – Continued Oppression in Freedom and the Early Struggles for Equality

The Civil War was instrumental in freeing African Americans from the literal chains that held them back. It meant no person could own another within the country, but that was only the beginning of a much longer and more difficult struggle for equality. It was easy to claim that justice had been served and no further action was needed since the slaves were freed.

With former slaves now making up a large percentage of the population near large plantations, Caucasians become unnerved and immediately began to look for ways to repress and re-enslave them. Being forced to release their slaves did not change the way slave owners viewed their former property; it meant they would have to be more creative in the ways they would repress an entire race.

Even in the Northern States, African Americans did not enjoy the same rights and privileges of their white counterparts. Northerners believed that no human should be owned, but they did not believe in an inherent equality, as was obvious by the way they treated other races and women. Though people focus on the inequality within Southern States, there was just as much inequality in the Northern States; it was simply more likely the codes and laws were unspoken. In recent history, some of the most racist laws have been enacted in Northern States, perhaps because only Southern States have been under adequate federal scrutiny. However, there is little doubt the majority of racist laws and statutes on the books (even if only in the past) were written and enforced in Southern States starting soon after the end of the Civil War.

Black Codes/Jim Crow Laws

Following the implementation of the 13th Amendment banning slavery in the country, authorities in the South began to look for ways to repress and ensure former slaves did not gain equal footing. As Reconstruction began in the South during 1865 and 1866, the Southern States began trying to assert States' rights over former slaves. Not only did they see African Americans as inferior beings, they feared the cost of having to pay former slaves would further hinder economic recovery. The result was the development of Black Codes, more commonly known as Jim Crow laws, which sought to restrict the rights of African Americans.

One such Black Code required former slaves to sign labor contracts to continue working on plantations. Any former slave who did not sign a contract could be arrested for vagrancy and either be fined or forced to work for free. Though not the only code, this was one of the harshest because it made it difficult for former slaves to find acceptable working conditions or move away. They were pressed to accept poor conditions barely better than those they experienced when they were slaves and to accept pay that was not adequate to live a better life just to avoid being jailed or forced into a "legal slavery."

The First Black Codes went into effect in South Carolina and Mississippi by the end of 1865. South Carolina limited the positions that African Americans could take, ensuring they could not advance economically or improve their situations. The only jobs that a former slave could take were as farmers and servants. An exception would be made for any African American willing to pay a tax of between $10 and $100 a year. As many former slaves worked as artisans or in cities, this made life nearly impossible to continue in the state where they resided. Because they could not prove their experience, they were not as valuable as those who had worked in these positions before. And with such a high tax, they could not continue doing what they knew how to do.

Some codes limited the kind of property that African Americans could own. Many said that African Americans could only testify in court when the case directly involved another African American. Children were forced to work when their parents couldn't, or if they did not have parents.

Though he was firmly on the side of the Union during the Civil War, President Andrew Johnson (who took office following Lincoln's assassination) strongly believed in States' rights. He did not believe it was within the federal government's right to undermine the Black Codes. Because of this, many in the Republican Party turned on him, and he would never be elected to the office that he held for four years. Still, considerable harm was done to the newly freed slaves because of his refusal to step in on their behalf.

14th and 15th Amendments

These amendments targeted the Southern States' resistance to treating former slaves as equals. It also forced Northern States to be more aware of their own biases. These amendments were meant to offset or negate many of the Black Codes passed in the South following the end of the Civil War.

The 14th Amendment tried to enforce the idea of equality.

> All persons born or naturalized in the United
> States and subject to the jurisdiction thereof,

are citizens of the United States and of the State wherein they reside. No State shall make or enforce any law which shall abridge the privileges or immunities of the citizens of the United States; nor shall any State deprive any person of life, liberty, or property, without due process of law; nor deny to any person within its jurisdiction the equal protection of the laws.

The amendment was ratified in 1868 and was meant to be enforced in the South to ensure all the basic rights guaranteed at the founding of the country were applied and granted to the former slaves (again, this was for men and many of the basic rights, such as voting, were still denied to all females).

The 15th Amendment was far more direct in what it sought to provide for African Americans. Southern States had already proved they were unwilling to ensure that all rights were granted, particularly the right to vote. This amendment focused specifically on that problem.

The right of citizens of the United States to vote shall not be denied or abridged by the United States or by any State on account of race, color, or previous condition of servitude.

The amendment was ratified in 1870. It specifically required Southern States to guarantee that all males would be allowed to vote, regardless of race.

Howard University

As former slaves fought for their basic rights, they began to band together when possible. One of their first successful endeavors was the founding of Howard University, the first African American university in the country. At a time when former slave owners sought to limit their potential, those African Americans who were educated and willing to share their knowledge to improve the situation of all former slaves began to fight back through education.

The university was founded in 1866 to train preachers. The intent of the university quickly morphed into much more, so that by May of 1867 it included medical training and courses in liberal arts. It sought to teach former slaves but also included white females who were the children of several of the founders. Established by Caucasians who wanted to further the potential and opportunities for former slaves, the school focused on elevating the way former slaves thought and helped to teach them how to navigate the inequality rampant everywhere.

Located in Washington, D.C., the school began to teach law. This helped to give former slaves the tools they needed to fight against the inequality established through the implementation of the Black Codes.

Reconstruction and After Effects

The period following the Civil War is called Reconstruction, and it lasted from 1867 to 1877. This period began with The Reconstruction Act of 1867. Those who were angered by President Johnson's unwillingness to secure the future of former slaves passed the act despite the President's veto.

The act required all Southern States to ratify the 14th Amendment. This meant those States would only be allowed to act as States within the union after guaranteeing they would follow the regulations for the equal protection of former slaves and the right to vote for all men (note that all women were still considered second-class citizens, and none had a right to vote). Because the President was unwilling to help the former slaves by claiming States' rights, this forced him to act to uphold the law.

Following the passage of the 15th Amendment, the right to vote gained an additional layer of protection. It had become clear that the Southern States were working to undermine voting for former slaves who would choose people who would pursue equality. During this time, African Americans were voted into all levels of government, including Congress.

Working to undermine everything being forced on them, many white supremacist organizations formed during Reconstruction, with the Ku Klux Klan being the most infamous. These groups gained increasing control. Following the exit of Northern assistance, these groups easily took over the now vulnerable governments, and they immediately began undoing all the gains inequality that had been won. Voting restrictions and laws that enforced inequality quickly went into effect, making it difficult for former slaves to make ends meet, let alone improve their dire circumstances. Though progress was made during this time, it was quickly squashed once the African American people were left without protection and the opportunities afforded them during the Reconstruction Period.

Hiram Revels

One of the most notable results of the passage of the 14th and 15th amendments was the short-lived opportunity that allowed African Americans to have a political say in government. As those in power in the South sought to curb the former slaves' ability to improve their situations, those same former slaves began using their ability to vote to put African Americans into government positions. The most impressive and historical achievement was that of Hiram Revels.

Revels was born a free man in North Carolina in 1827. He became a preacher, an occupation that would prove instrumental to his future career. Traveling around the nation during the 1840s and 1850s, he saw the plight and potential of African Americans. His Christian preaching was only part of his plan – he also sought to teach and train other freemen. Revels even put his own safety at risk when he moved to Missouri, which had a law that forbade any freemen from residing in the state. Revels admitted that he had to be particularly cautious during his time in St. Louis, but he showed that his primary purpose was passing on the word of the Gospel, not instigating rebellion or encouraging slaves to escape. In 1854, the state imprisoned him, which led to his departure as soon as he was released. His next destination was Maryland.

When the Civil War began, he helped to recruit soldiers for the African American regiments within his current state of residence. He himself acted as the chaplain.

By 1870, Revels had moved to Mississippi, where several African Americans had been elected to government positions in the state legislature. They felt it was time to press for someone even more visible. The result was Revels winning a Congressional seat in the U.S. Senate. Mississippi had not been officially readmitted to the union yet, so upon his arrival in Washington, D.C., Revels had to wait for final approval to take his position. He was filling the seat vacated by Jefferson Davis, the former President of the Confederacy who clearly was not allowed to serve in the Senate following his treasonous actions. Because Revels was taking over the remainder of Davis's term, he was a Senator for 2 years (1869 to 1871).

Revels did not consider himself a representative of his race, but of his state and country. He pointed out the problems both within the Southern States and the less acknowledged problems in the Northern States, demonstrating that the blame did not lay in a single location but with institutions across the entire country. He often fought to help African Americans in the South earn the ability to be educated.

Revels also appealed an unfair ban of African American mechanics on working at the US Navy Yard in the city of Baltimore.

Though his time in the Senate was short, Revels could prove just how much an African American could do to break down problems. Many lauded his exceptional oratory skills. His desire for equality through peaceful means was an inspiration, and his willingness to risk his own safety helped pave the way for the Civil Rights Movement nearly 100 years later.

Chapter 7 – Exodus from the South and the Fight for Education within the South

Once Reconstruction ended, the situation worsened significantly for the former slaves who continued to live in the Southern States. The people had come down to help rebuild the South and ensure that equality was extended to all who were no longer there. Though they had meant well, the people who had worked during Reconstruction had failed in their efforts in several significant ways. The withdrawal of federal support would have long-lasting consequences for the region.

The three amendments following the end of the Civil War (13th, 14th, and 15th) could be manipulated and laws contorted to work around actually providing former slaves with their basic rights. It did not take long for the former slave owners and those in power to start eroding all the steps toward equality that had been taken, leaving African Americans vulnerable and desperate. Knowing that they would not find the kind of life promised them by the Constitution and its amendments, many chose to leave the Southern States instead of trying to work within a system that was perpetually constrictive and cruel.

Kansas Migration

The largest exodus of African Americans is known as the Kansas Migration or the Exodus to Kansas. With the rise of Black Codes meant to keep them down, many former slaves decided that it was best to simply leave than to be forced into a life that was only slightly better than slavery. In Kansas, they believed they would be able to choose their own vocation and work to improve their situations.

By the spring of 1879, thousands of former slaves had decided to make a move rather than to continue in their oppressive situations. The number of injustices and growing systemic racism that governed the Southern States ensured that those who could leave would do so. Slaves could no longer believe in the country that had promised one thing only to engulf them in another type of slavery that was much harder to fight against. With hope all but gone, thousands of former slaves packed up their belongings and left for a place they thought could provide more opportunities and equality. The state with the most promise was not a Northern state, but a state to the west. Though this state had earned a dubious name prior to the start of the Civil War (Bleeding Kansas because of the riots and rebellions over whether slavery should be allowed there), it looked promising to many former slaves.

It is likely former slaves remembered the fervor of John Brown and the fight to have a free Kansas, one of the harbingers of the Civil War, which proved to be the end of physical slavery.

This also meant that the Southern States lost many of the former slaves who could have been the greatest benefit to them. African Americans thought of Kansas as a refuge, a place of promise. It was certainly an idealized and romanticized version of the state, which had just as many negative as positive aspects to endorse it. However, there was no doubt that remaining in the Southern States would result in misery and suffering. Kansas was a promise of something better, no matter how small the improvement was.

This was the first time that so many African Americans had the ability to choose their residence, and they took advantage of their new freedom. This was a huge blow to the Southern States, not only because they lost a number of laborers, but also because they lost many of the brightest minds that could have helped them move forward. Very few who had the choice to leave stayed in the increasingly volatile and precarious position of being a former slave in a state where they were freed only after a four-year war. Those in power were eager to prove that slavery was over only because the South had lost – in no other way would they allow former slaves to live free and happy.

As a result, many Southerners began blaming the North for interfering, saying their labor force was being lured away, even though it was clear the problem was because of their own actions. The former slaves were not heading North. A Senate committee was established to determine the truth of the allegations, and the final findings of that investigation pointed to what was already obvious; the oppression and injustices of the Southern States were the problems, not any outside factors.

Ironically, the biggest proponents of the former slaves remaining in the Southern States were educated Northern African Americans. They felt the former slaves were little better than children who did not know what was in their best interest. They believed they could guide the Southern African Americans, creating the equality they falsely believed thrived in the Northern States.

The former slaves rejected the condescending and unrealistic beliefs of the African American elites of the North who clearly did not understand the real situation. Both the North and South were shocked to find they could not stem the exodus. The South had expected they would be able to force their former slaves to live as they had previously lived, failing to grasp the fact that African

Americans were no longer slaves. The freed slaves could leave, choosing an uncertain and perilous path over the oppression of their former masters. The people from the Northern States were just as shocked because they could not believe the former slaves would choose not to listen to them. Having abandoned African Americans in the South after Reconstruction, there was no reason for the former slaves to listen to them. It was impossible for the North to grasp just how terrible the situation was as they were busy congratulating themselves for creating an equal nation without paying attention to the reality of the situation.

Benjamin Singleton and Henry Adams

With no support from any government officials or established leaders, uneducated African Americans who had strong leadership skills led the migration. Benjamin Singleton and Henry Adams (from Tennessee and Louisiana, respectively) organized assistance within their States for those who wished to leave.

Benjamin Singleton had been a slave who managed to escape with the Underground Railroad. After the Civil War ended, he returned to the state where he had been enslaved and began to work. As a trained carpenter, he was skilled and capable. His time on the Underground Railroad had also taught him about leadership. As he had learned to make coffins, he was too often exposed to the cruel fate of African Americans at the hands of former Confederates.

Unable to keep quiet or still, he founded the Tennessee Real Estate & Homestead Association. The primary objective was to help African Americans leave the deplorable conditions of Tennessee to seek a better life in Kansas.

Henry Adams served in the Army, and his medical skills and accomplishments earned him respect from both African Americans and Caucasians in Louisiana. He joined the Colored Men's

Protective Union once he was out of the Army. The organization's purpose was to analyze the living conditions of African Americans and determine a way to improve them. The result of their observations and analysis was that former Confederates would not allow for the equality of African Americans, let alone improvements to their situations. Deciding that former Confederates were re-creating slavery in the closest possible ways without the actual institution, they contacted President Rutherford B. Hayes and Congress to request assistance. If the federal government could not offer them protection from the pervasive inequality and injustice inflicted by former Confederates, the organization requested an area be set apart for former slaves to start new lives, or to prepare ships that would take former slaves to Liberia. Nearly 100,000 African Americans had signed on saying they were interested in relocating. Adams presented these findings and requests to the Senate.

When the government failed them, the organization helped to relocate as many people as possible to Kansas. However, the American Colonization Society was founded in 1882, and it helped to relocate roughly 12,000 former slaves to Liberia.

Spelman College

While the federal government worked to make sure African American men were treated equally, African American women were largely ignored. In 1881, this began to change with the founding of Spelman College. Sophia B. Packard and Harriet E. Giles founded the school in Atlanta as a way of providing opportunities for African American women. It started in the basement of a church with two teachers and 11 students. The school began specifically to help educate former female slaves. Although they had only a few students, Packard and Giles dreamed of creating a school that would champion liberal arts, which meant they had a long way to take their mostly illiterate students. It was a particularly difficult path, but one that the founders were determined to walk.

One of the earliest patrons of the school was John D. Rockefeller who pledged $250 to the school in 1882. By 1883, the school had to move from the basement. Purchasing nine acres of land, the school had five buildings from which to teach the women who attended the Spelman.

The first class to graduate from the school earned a high school diploma in 1887.

Booker T Washington

Born a slave in 1856, Booker Taliaferro Washington was the child of a slave and her master (whom he never met). Still young at the end of the Civil War, Washington worked manual labor jobs. Despite working, he did attend school part-time in West Virginia until he was 16 years old. He enrolled and entered Hampton Institute after completing his early education. Working as a janitor to pay for room and board, Washington's tuition was paid for by the school's principal friend. He went on to teach others at Hampton, Malden, and Hampton Institute.

As his abilities became more well known, he was given the opportunity to construct and organize a school for African Americans at the Tuskegee Institute in Alabama. This was partly in response to the Kansas Migration and was considered as a way of mitigating it. The Institute was trying to offer a way to educate former slaves so that they could reach their full potential. He believed that African Americans needed to strive for economic improvement before pressing for equality. Because of this, he was an outspoken and key advocate for businesses founded by African Americans or that sought to improve their positions.

In 1895, he gave a polarizing speech in Atlanta in acknowledgment of the increase in lynchings in the South. In this speech, he pressed for African Americans to focus on gaining economic stability instead of fighting against the increasing number of Jim Crow laws being passed. Though the laws made it more difficult to find economic stability, fighting for legal equality was proving to be far more dangerous. He sent people to help establish better economic conditions in the Southern States.

Despite his speech and the backlash he received from former slaves and Northerners, Washington was taking action to stem and remove Jim Crow laws. He did so in secret so it would not look like he was undermining the compromise he tried to broker in his speech.

George Washington Carver

Like Booker T. Washington, George Washington Carver was born into slavery. His mother died or was abducted when he was very young, but the family who had kept her chose to raise her son as one of their own. Living in Missouri, he was educated by the family and eventually went to Iowa State College where he got his master's degree in 1896.

Following his graduation, Carver took a position with the Tuskegee Institute and remained there for almost 20 years. Beyond his teachings, Carver was a remarkable inventor and innovator. He could derive numerous uses for common crops, with peanuts being the most famous.

He knew and worked with Booker T. Washington, and though he was less well-known during their lifetime, his intelligence, quiet demeanor, and inventiveness turned him into a legend who is better known than nearly any other African American of his time.

Plessy versus Ferguson

One of the greatest miscarriages of justice in U.S. History occurred in 1896, and it was based on the obvious fallacy that separate could be equal.

The case started in 1892 when Homer Plessy decided he was not going to follow the Jim Crow law that said African Americans had to sit in a car designated for them on a train. Plessy argued that his basic rights were being denied when he was forced to sit in one car over another simply based on the color of his skin.

Unfortunately, the Supreme Court set a dangerous and reckless precedent that Jim Crow laws, which created an environment of racial discrimination, were not contrary to the Constitution or 14th Amendment. Essentially, they said that States were within their rights to keep races separate in public if African Americans were given something roughly equal to what Caucasians had. This law would hamper economic and societal growth for African Americans for more than half a century. It wasn't until 1954 that this miscarriage of justice was overturned in Brown versus Board of Education of Topeka (Chapter 5).

Chapter 8 – African Americans Begin to Stand Together

While there were many movements to help African Americans, they were usually small and focused on helping small groups or areas where the African-American populations were high. By the beginning of the 20th century, African Americans started to come together to create much larger groups and organizations, reaching out to a wider audience. A number of schools had also been founded, but they did not have enough backing to reach those who needed education the most.

Several organizations formed in response to the increasingly oppressive and cruel Jim Crow laws and the lesser acknowledged racism prevalent in the Northern States.

Niagara Movement

It is perhaps ironic that one of the first large movements against racism within the U.S. stemmed not from issues in the South, but blatant racism in the North. Although it is called the Niagara Movement, it was actually a group of civil rights activists who decided to stand up after a racist incident in Buffalo, New York.

In 1904, 29 African Americans from numerous fields (including teachers, business owners, and clergymen) attempted to enter a hotel in Buffalo and were denied admittance. As a result, the group of

African Americans who were denied admittance in Buffalo went to Niagara Falls and convened. Their goal was to fight the kind of discrimination that they had faced in Buffalo.

The two most well-known members and founders were W.E.B. DuBois and William Monroe Trotter. Both felt that the compromise touted by Booker T. Washington, in his speech in Atlanta, was a step backward for African Americans. They wanted to push civil rights to the forefront of public debate.

The result of the first meeting was the "Declaration of Principles." This declaration said that it was wrong to expect African Americans to accept a position of inferiority when they had been promised the same inalienable rights as Caucasians. It was impossible to treat an entire race of people as being inferior and still provide them the same rights, something that occurred daily throughout the Southern states but, as what happened to them at the hotel in Buffalo, was also present in the North.

Countering Washington's stated desire to ignore the legal aspect for now to pursue economic prosperity, the Niagara Movement focused almost exclusively on legal cases. Their work included fighting inequality in economics, health, education, religion, and crime.

Though it was not the first African American organization, it was the first to wield any real power. They were unequivocal in their demands for equality in society and opportunities. However, one of the biggest divides within the organization was the disagreement between the two primary founding members. W.E.B. DuBois insisted that the right to vote should be protected not only for African American males, but that it should be extended to all women. Willian Monroe Trotter was against this as he agreed with the patriarchy and was willing to compromise on what women should be allowed to do. In 1908, he left the Niagara Movement to found his own organization, the Negro-American Political League.

Between 1904 and 1908, the organization met annually. However, the nation's first racial riot erupted in 1908, during a meeting of the group in Illinois. Eight African Americans were killed and more than 2,000 were forced to flee the city. Given that the first racial riot occurred in the hometown of Abraham Lincoln, many people began to view the plight of African Americans in a much different light. It was becoming increasingly obvious that the problem was not merely with the Southern States, but with the country as a whole.

Trotter's Negro-American Political League eventually dissolved and its name and tenets largely unmentioned in the history books, while DuBois would go on to be one of the founding members of the National Association for the Advancement of Colored People.

National Association for the Advancement of Colored People

Once it became clear that a much stronger, more unified, and easy to recognize organization was required to help African Americans, several members of the Niagara Movement began to form an organization that became far more powerful. However, it wasn't just members of the Niagara Movement who were appalled by what the race riot exhibited. Coupled with the growing trend of lynchings in the South, several Caucasian liberals decided that the system was not on its way to repairing the damage that slavery and the Civil War had done to the country as they previously had believed. The result of the combined efforts of African American leaders and Caucasian liberals was the formation of the National Association for the Advancement of Colored People, known today as the NAACP.

Among the most notable founding members in addition to DuBois were Ida B. Wells-Barnett, Mary Church Terrell, Mary White Ovington, Oswald Garrison Villard, William English Walling, and Dr. Henry Moscowitz. On the centennial of the birth of Abraham Lincoln, 60 people called for a meeting to determine how to address the obvious and rampant injustices against African Americans. Following the path started by the Niagara Movement, the expressed purpose of the newly formed organization was to ensure the rights of all US citizens under the 13th, 14th, and 15th Amendments.

Beyond that purpose, the new organization wanted to ensure that African Americans would have as many opportunities and as much potential to achieve the American dream as their Caucasian counterparts. This would require they fight inequality and racial barriers across the nation, not just within small areas or regions of the country. Compromises of any sort would hinder progress on all fronts.

Learning that the annual meetings of the Niagara Movement were not adequate to properly fight the root problems, the NAACP finally established a headquarters in 1910 in New York City. Nearly everyone on the board of directors and legal staff was a Caucasian male. The sole exception was the director of publications and research, a position that was offered to DuBois, which he accepted. That same year, he started *The Crisis*, the official journal of the organization.

The Crisis and W.E.B DuBois

Today, his journal is one of the oldest and most well-respected African American publications. Over the years, it evolved from addressing problems within the country to celebrating African American culture. It was instrumental in the progress and boom known as the Harlem Renaissance as DuBois published works by some of the most renowned artists of the artistic movement.

Over time, the publication also became a way to discuss issues and debate solutions to current problems. There are poems, essays, works of fiction, and other literary achievements in the journal, as well as writings on how to resolve many of the problems still prevalent in American society.

Universal Negro Improvement Association and Marcus Garvey

Unlike the other two organizations, the Universal Negro Improvement Association did not seek to better African American life; rather it sought to return African Americans to Africa. The primary proponent of association was Marcus Garvey.

Another difference between this organization and the others is that it attracted a considerable amount of international attention. In places like Canada and the Caribbean, nations that had been marred by the institution of slavery, a growing number of people were interested in determining whether the solutions offered by Marcus Garvey could in fact improve their lives.

Garvey combined both politics and religion in the organization. In his "Declaration of Rights of the Negro Peoples of the World," Garvey believed that he was providing a religious path forward for everyone of African descent. Their motto made it clear that the organization sought more than just equality: "One God! One Aim! One Destiny!" It was the belief of the organization that the right path forward could only be found through God, and that he would lead those of African descent to the successful lives they sought, including their own independence.

Garvey drew considerable inspiration from Booker T. Washington. Following the professed belief of Washington that African Americans needed to prove that they deserved equal rights, Garvey firmly believed that self-help was the only way forward for them. The result was the founding of the Universal Negro Improvement Association in 1914.

Over time, that belief changed. The increased number of lynchings, the perpetual oppression of Jim Crow laws, and the unwillingness of "good people" to acknowledge the problem (let alone fix it), caused a change in Garvey's beliefs. He lost his faith that self-help was the answer. By the time World War I ended, Garvey had seen how those of African descent were used for the most dangerous and deadly jobs, but received almost no recognition for their bravery and sacrifice. Several race riots broke out between 1917 and 1919. It had become clear to Garvey that nothing those of African descent did would ever be enough to cause Caucasians to view them as equals.

Believing that integration would never work, Garvey and his organization began to seek a way to return those of African descent to a place where they could control their own destinies. His dream was the formation of an independent nation in Africa that would be governed by those who had been oppressed following the fall of slavery.

Garvey viewed the perceptions of African Americans of themselves as the biggest obstacle to his dream. They first had to find the strength to fight for themselves, as he proclaimed in one of the meetings: "If you want liberty, you yourselves must strike the blow. If you must be free, you must become so through your own effort." He tried to get them to take pride and ownership of their heritage, not to hide it so that they could try to blend into a society that had proved it was unwilling to accept them.

His views were often at odds with the NAACP. DuBois went so far as to call him, "the most dangerous enemy of the Negro race in America and in the world," because Garvey sought to segregate those of African descent by moving them to another continent. Having earned animosity with both those seeking to gain equality and the federal government, Garvey was imprisoned in 1922 for mail fraud. He was deported to Jamaica in 1925 following his release from prison. After his deportation, the organization lost most of its momentum and slid into obscurity.

Chapter 9 – Founding of Something New Through Pain and Self-Expression

Art has always been one of the greatest ways of expressing a sense of self, whether as an individual or for an entire race. Unable to find equality and safety in a nation that treated them like a sub-class of humans, African Americans found their own means of expression through art. One of the most famous African-American poets came out of this need for expression - Langston Hughes. There were also several famous artists who used their works to express the plight of African Americans. However, the best-known form of expression with the most long-lasting effects occurred in music. The influence of the African American innovation in music has created numerous genres, many of which are well respected and beloved around the world.

The Harlem Renaissance – Expression of the African American Experience

Regardless of where they lived, African Americans found they never had the same chance to achieve the American Dream. From the deep South where the slightest misstep could result in lynching to the hearts of Northern cities where they were hidden in the slums, there were only a few ways that an African American could find success. The 1920s to 1930s saw the result of decades of broken promises following the Civil War – a single united voice of pain, suffering, and a new hope. It was a time of new and original art rising from the depths of the African American soul – the Harlem Renaissance.

This was the heart and experience of a people with a stolen history trapped in a world that offered limited opportunities. It was a time when they expressed who they were beyond those experiences. They were not sub-humans or second-class citizens; they were artists and intellectuals who had finally found their voice.

The Harlem Renaissance is called the "spiritual coming of age" for an entire generation of African Americans realizing they deserved more than they were getting. Disillusioned after the failure of the Civil War to bring about equality, they felt compelled to show the nation in which they lived who they were. The result was several new genres of artistic expression.

At the core of this movement were Langston Hughes, Wallace Thurman, Countee Cullan, Nella Larsen, Jessie Remon Fauset, Jean Toomer, Arna Bontemps, and Zora Neale Hurston.

Ironically, it was the curiosity of Caucasians who were interested in the new and exotic look and feel emanating from this new artistic expression that shone a light on the movement. This allowed it to grow, spread, and evolve over time. One of their favorites from this period was the blunt beauty of the poetry by Langston Hughes. However, the purpose of the art during this period was not meant as a political statement – it was pure self-expression and a retelling of their experience, just like the Italian Renaissance. The ideas had been taking shape for decades and had finally found the right spiritual and intellectual ground to take shape.

Langston Hughes

Easily one of the most famous American poets, Langston Hughes had an appeal that went well beyond the experience of a single person or race. He had a way with words that could speak to nearly anyone.

Born in Missouri in 1902, Hughes was raised by his grandmother after his parents divorced. When his mother remarried, Hughes moved in with her and her new husband in Lincoln, Illinois, at the age of 13. This was when he began to write poetry. Once he finished high school, he spent a year in Mexico, and then attended Columbia University in New York City; however, he did not graduate. He traveled for a while and finally settled briefly in Washington, D.C., where his first book of poetry was published, in 1926. He would then move to Pennsylvania to earn his degree at Lincoln University.

His first successful literary endeavor was in 1930 when he published his first novel titled, *Not Without Laughter*. The novel would go on to win the Harmon Gold Medal. Though he is best known for his poetry, Hughes first gained recognition for his novels. Among his literary influences, including Carl Sandburg and Walt Whitman, Hughes also found inspiration in the new musical genre called Jazz.

One of the reasons he is the best-known artist from the Harlem Renaissance was precisely because he did not treat his personal life as a political statement. He did not divide his work into a representation of the African American experience and his own experience. To Hughes, he was simply an American whose works reflected his own experiences, which were like those of the average African American, so he did not feel he needed to expound upon or highlight the lives of others. Nor did he feel he could speak for others. He wrote for African Americans, not America. Hughes used images and ideas that would appeal to those who had experienced it. The fact it also appealed to Caucasians showed that, while there were many ways in which the American experience differed based on a person's race, some elements were universal. Over the course of his life, Hughes would tour the country reading his poetry; very likely surpassing any other American in terms of the number of people who heard him read his own works.

Zora Neale Hurston

Though not as well known today as Langston Hughes, Zora Neale Hurston was a literary giant in her day. Still considered to be one of the most influential writers in the U.S., she had humble beginnings.

Born in 1891, Hurston's birthplace is debated; some say she was born in Alabama, but she claimed to have been born in Florida. It is believed she was born in Alabama but that her earliest memories were of living in Florida because her family moved there when she was an infant or toddler. Even her birth date is debated. What is known is that both of her parents were slaves who were freed following the end of the Civil War. Her mother died when she was young, and her father remarried. As a result, she moved around to live with several families during her early years.

After working odd jobs, Hurston finally earned an associate's degree at Howard University. She also published her first work in a small newspaper run by the university. From there, she moved to Harlem in New York City. It was there she would become one of the most well-known members of the Harlem Renaissance.

Intrigued by the experience of people of African descent in the Americas, she traveled as a young adult around the Southern U.S., Latin American, and the Caribbean. The result of her travels was her first book titled, *Mules and Men*. In 1937, she published the book that is often considered her masterpiece, *Their Eyes Were Watching God*. To this day, it is still used in schools to show resilience in the face of adversity as the story follows a young girl of mixed race from her early teenage years through later adulthood.

The Draw and Beauty of Jazz

One of the earliest forms of American music, Jazz, got its start in New Orleans. It evolved out of the Blues genre, but had a much more vibrant and hopeful sound than its source. Unlike a lot of cities in the South, New Orleans was a melting pot of many different cultures, and even its name shows that it has a distinctly different heritage to the other major cities in the country.

Jazz began as a way of expressing life as an African American. It was oppressed and nervous, yet upbeat and optimistic. There are so many facets and types of jazz because it conveys a unique range of emotions. This has made it one of the most popular and expressive forms of music within the U.S. Mixing the African American experience and rhythms with the styles of religious music, Jazz has a mass appeal that has kept the attention and focus of a nation even to the present day.

Rock and Roll would later be born from a combination of Jazz and Folk Music. Beyond that, jazz musicians were the ones to design the first drum set. The influence this genre has had on the musical world is groundbreaking and breathtaking.

Ginger Smock – A Female Star in a Masculine Industry

Jazz had mass appeal, but across the nation, men dominated the news for this genre. Ginger Smock was one of only a few women able to break into the male-dominated world, and she did it in the highly competitive city of Los Angeles, California. Born in Chicago in 1920, her parents died when she was only six. Her aunt and uncle adopted her and brought her to LA.

It was soon obvious that she was both intrigued by, and highly skilled in, music. Her talent was so extraordinary that her adopted parents signed her up for private music lessons so that she could learn to play the violin. By ten years old, she had already performed at the Hollywood Bowl, and the next year held a solo recital at a Los Angeles's First AME Church. Throughout her teenage years, she gained more popularity and renown, including playing for the LA Junior Philharmonic, where she was the only African American performer.

In 1943, she became the protégé of Stuff Smith, an influential jazz musician. Smock had long been intrigued by jazz and had done her own improvisations inspired by the musical genre. Smith moved her from the classical world to the jazz world, booking a professional job in Southern California with the Sepia Tones, a trio of women performers.

After World War II began, her chance to shine in the male-dominated industry arrived. With many men being sent to war, bands and clubs became desperate for talent, and they could not have found a more professional and talented performer than Smock. Even after the war ended, she was in demand. During 1957, she had her own TV show called *Rhythm Review* and went on to do numerous recordings for professional studios. She eventually faded from the public eye as rock and roll gained in popularity and musical instruments were abandoned for the newer sound and fresher faces.

Louis Armstrong – The Face and Sound of Jazz

It is impossible to talk about Jazz without talking about Louis Armstrong. From his deep, rich voice to his unparalleled trumpet skills, Armstrong became the living embodiment of the joys and sorrows of Jazz.

Born in 1901 in New Orleans, Armstrong had a difficult childhood. His father left the family after he was born, and his mother often left him with her parents. He was forced to leave school to work before he finished the fifth grade.

The Karnofsky family gave him work and noticed his beautiful voice. They encouraged him to sing and frequently had him join them at their evening meals. This would not last long as he found his stepfather's gun and shot it into the air in celebration of New Year's in 1912. Armstrong was arrested and sent away to the Colored Waif's Home for Boys.

This was a turning point for him because he fell in love with playing music. Drawn to the cornet, it was the beginning of one of the most beautiful jazz careers in the U.S. Initially, Armstrong played the blues, a genre that sounded amazing on the cornet and trumpet. He found a mentor and would become a substitute for Joe "King" Oliver.

By 1922, jazz had taken off in New Orleans, and for Armstrong it was an easy transition from the blues to the more upbeat genre. He was invited to play in Chicago with his cornet, and he immediately accepted. In 1923, he made his first recording. During the next few years, he managed to learn and improvise swing music, which he would then introduce to the Fletcher Henderson's Orchestra. The mix of sounds resulted in the world's first jazz big band, and it influenced the sounds and music of the next two decades.

He would leave the Henderson's because his Southern upbringing and background was considered too coarse. Additionally, Henderson would not allow him to sing, thinking that the harsher sound would not be welcome by the more refined audience.

This turned out to be a springboard for Armstrong. Returning to Chicago, he was given his first recording with his own band, called Louis Armstrong and His Hot Five. The recordings over the next three years are regarded among the most influential recordings in the history of jazz. It was also the beginning of his singing career, which resulted in the founding of scat singing.

The public loved him, but critics seemed to loathe Armstrong. Uncaring of the negative reviews, Armstrong went on to tour in Europe and gained in popularity abroad.

Though he had a rocky career, including ties to several mobs, Armstrong persisted because of his love of music. He would write the first African-American jazz autobiography (*Swing That Music*) and be the first African-American performer to get a feature billing in a large Hollywood movie (*Pennies from Heaven*). His personal life was equally troubled, but he finally settled down in 1943 with his fourth wife. Seeing that his music was becoming less popular, he began playing in more intimate and relaxed settings. Those who played with him would rotate over the years, but it seemed to be a time of greater peace for the musical legend.

During the 1950s, there was a renewed interest in his musical talent, and he would go on to join numerous artists on their recordings and release several new albums (often regarded as some of his best music), including the Jazz version of "Mack the Knife." During this time, his international popularity experienced a resurgence, earning him the name "Ambassador Satch."

However, jazz continued to evolve and newer musicians, such as Miles Davis, and Dizzy Gillespie, saw Armstrong as being too old-fashioned for the direction they wanted to take this genre. Their sound was meant to be artistic, not entertaining, and they did not like his stage presence that focused on entertaining everyone, and not expressing himself. His refusal to talk openly about the systemic racism and struggle of African Americans further distanced him from the new trends in jazz.

All that changed in 1957 when he witnessed the Arkansas Governor deploying the National Guard to block nine African-American students from being integrated into the school. Irate after the incident, Armstrong was astonishingly critical of the way the President appeared to let a state governor break the law. His statements were front-page news in the U.S. and around the world. The same people who had criticized him for remaining silent were now strangely silent themselves, leaving Armstrong to be the face of transparent indignation for the racism in the U.S. It has earned him a place in history because he was open about his feelings during a crisis where many chose to be silent.

His music career continued to flourish for the remainder of his life. One of his most famous songs, "What a Wonderful World", was recorded in 1967. He died in 1971.

Ella Fitzgerald

Just as one must talk about Louis Armstrong when discussing the history of jazz, one must also discuss the amazing and lasting influence of Ella Fitzgerald. She is still known as "The First Lady of Song" because of her unbelievable vocal range and emotional skills.

Born in 1917 in Newport News, VA, Ella moved to Yonkers, New York, when she was young. Her mother moved in with her long-time boyfriend, Joseph Da Silva. Though he was not Ella's father, he helped to raise her. She was a friendly child who could befriend anyone in the mixed neighborhood in which her family lived. She worked running bets and money for local gamblers (though she probably did not understand the business that she assisted) and considered herself a tomboy.

The first real problem in her life occurred in 1932 when her mother, Tempie, died in a car accident. Ella stayed with her stepfather briefly after the loss of her mother, but soon moved in with her mother's sister back in Virginia. Her half-sister would join her soon after when Ella's stepfather died of a heart attack. She did not like her school and would frequently skip out. After some trouble with the police, Fitzgerald was sent to a reform school where she was abused.

At 15, Ella escaped from the school and entered the cruel world during the Great Depression. These difficult years helped to form her vocal range because she could draw from the pain she experienced to better express a wider range of emotions.

She had her first break in 1934 when she won a drawing at the Apollo to perform. Initially, her plan was to dance, but the performers before her intimidated the young woman. Uncertain and flustered, she stood on the stage and was initially booed for her silence. Finally coming out of her shock, she requested that the house band play "Judy", a song that she loved to listen to with her mother. The skeptical crowd was soon stunned into silence as her voice took over the venue. As soon as she finished, the crowd demanded a second song, and she happily obliged.

Fitzgerald's on-stage persona was completely different from her offstage personality. She seemed confident and fearless, a stark contrast to the shy woman she had become after several years of misfortune.

Seeing how difficult it was for her, and realizing she had a lot of raw talent, the saxophonist for the house band helped her launch her career, introducing her to people who could move her singing forward.

In 1935, she began to sing jazz songs, where she really found the right genre for her impressive range and talent. She learned to sing scat, taking Armstrong's course work and turning it into a masterful work of art. She went on to become a favorite for many popular shows, such as the Bing Crosby, Frank Sinatra, and Ed Sullivan Shows.

Fitzgerald's manager refused to put up with any discrimination by any establishment while his star was touring. His attitude created friction when they toured in the South, and during one tour in Dallas, Fitzgerald, Dizzy Gillespie, and Illinois Jacquet were arrested. She would later recount her disgust that the police hauled them off to jail and then asked for their autographs.

In the 1950s, Marilyn Monroe helped to further break down the racial barrier that kept Fitzgerald out of some of the most popular nightclubs. Monroe requested that Fitzgerald is allowed to perform at the Mocambo – in return, she told the owner she would sit visibly in the front of the club to watch Fitzgerald perform. Naturally, the press came to see Marilyn so publically enjoying a show, but they ended up publishing a story on Fitzgerald. This fortunate event ensured the legend would never have to take small jobs for the rest of her career.

Now part of the mainstream in terms of popularity, Fitzgerald became a world-renowned singer. She toured around the world singing, even though it had an adverse effect on her health.

One of her personal passions was child welfare, and she spent a considerable amount of money trying to help organizations that focused on youths. Because of this, she continued to push herself to work longer and harder, further harming her health. She was awarded the National Medal of Arts in 1987 and several other honorary degrees, including from Yale and Dartmouth. She died in 1996.

Jackie Robinson

The art inspired by the Harlem Renaissance was singular and inspirational, but it was not the only form of entertainment and expression. Nor was it the most obvious way of integrating African Americans into the rest of America. While the Harlem Renaissance expressed the African American experience, Jackie Robinson looked to use his talents to change the problems that plagued the nation. During a time when the nation tried to keep the races segregated, Jackie Robinson sought to break down the barriers.

An exceptional athlete, Jack Roosevelt Robinson came from humble beginnings. Born in 1919 in Cairo, Georgia, he was raised by his mother. As the only African American family in their area, Robinson and his four siblings were often faced with racism and discrimination. Undeterred, he began playing sports. His brother was in the Olympics, and Robinson wanted to follow his brother's example, and met with considerable success. He was talented at all the sports that he played while at UCLA.

In the Army, he quickly became frustrated by the discrimination within the military. He refused to move to the back of a bus and was arrested. Although he was court-martialed, Robinson eventually received an honorable discharge.

With his impeccable character and reputation, Robinson caught the eye of Branch Rickey, the manager of the Brooklyn Dodgers, in 1947. Robinson did not disappoint his new team either. Despite the anger of fans and players at an African American being integrated into the team, Robinson's performance was impossible to deny. He not only received the first rookie of the year award, but he was also the first person to steal every base in a game. In 1955, he was instrumental in the Dodgers winning the World Series against the New York Yankees. He took the team from being one of the biggest jokes in baseball to one of the greatest triumphs in the history of the sport. He did all this while being subjected to jeers and boos of the crowds. When they booed him, Robinson responded with a better performance, proving why he was in the stadium with the rest of the team.

While the artists were busy reflecting and expressing, Robinson was actively working to remove the laws and barriers that caused the pain experienced and expressed by those artists. His willingness to tolerate the cruelty of the crowd became a symbol for strength of character and the image of determination in the face of adversity.

Chapter 10 – Integration and the Civil Rights Movement

By the middle of the 20ᵗʰ century, African Americans were beginning to act to reduce and eliminate the discrimination they had suffered since the end of the Civil War. With Jim Crow laws and lynching being a persistent problem in the Southeastern States, while slums and barely masked racism were common in the Northeastern States, it became clear the fight for equality had to be waged on a national level. Clearly, there were areas of the country that required a much stronger presence, but the focus could not be contained to a single region. To gain equality, African Americans needed to be treated as equals regardless of where they lived.

From this understanding, began the Civil Rights Movement. Owing to the ideas and works of people like Booker T. Washington, Washington Carver, and W.E.B. DuBois, a growing number of leaders rose to help push the plight of African Americans to the forefront of public consciousness. The movement grew out of daily struggles, but it was punctuated by several notable events in U.S. History.

African Americans in the Military
While many Caucasian Americans wanted to deny there was a problem in the Northeast, claiming that the problem was mostly in

the Southeastern States, a look at the treatment of African Americans in the U.S. Military proved that the Civil Rights violations were a national problem.

African Americans have actively participated in every major war in U.S. history, but they were never treated as equals with their Caucasian counterparts, nor were they recognized for their sacrifices. Instead they were expected to be satisfied while being treated as inferior soldiers, enduring segregation like Jackie Robinson and accepting substandard supplies and living conditions. Their units were provided with fewer and lesser quality materials and received less attention during times of peace and war. It was only in 1948 when President Harry S. Truman signed an executive order requiring the military to be integrated that things started to change and improve.

Over time, recognition has been given to past African American units and military personnel for their contributions.

One such unit was the 54th Massachusetts Infantry. The first African American unit formed to fight with the Union forces during the Civil War, exemplified courage in the face of the impossible. Assigned with the dangerous task of leading the charge against the Confederate fort, Battery Wagner (Fort Wagner), in 1863, the company charged into battle. When the colonel was killed, Sergeant William H. Carney took up the American flag and led the attack to take a small portion of the fort. They would soon be called to retreat, and Sergeant Carney picked up the flag again as the others retreated. He was shot twice, but survived the battle. In 1900 (nearly 40 years after the battle), he was awarded the Congressional Medal of Honor for his bravery, becoming the first African American to receive the medal.

During World War II, the Tuskegee Airmen earned a place in history as the first African Americans in military aviation. The program was initiated at the Tuskegee Institute, although it was a source of outrage for African Americans who still saw this as the federal government perpetuating the inequality inherent with segregation. In 1943, the first Tuskegee pilots joined the Allies in Northern Africa, forming the 99th Fighter Squadron. Working with the Caucasian 79th Fighter Group, the pilots showed the potential of full integration within the military.

Brown vs. Board of Education of Topeka Kansas

The Jim Crow laws did not see any serious challenge or risk of cessation until 1954, when the case of segregation in schools reached the U.S. Supreme Court. The case was Brown vs. Board of Education of Topeka Kansas and it directly questioned the idea that government regulated institutions could be truly equal if they were separate. Although the same question had been put before the US Supreme Court in 1896 in the Plessy vs. Ferguson case, many events had occurred to prove that the theory did not hold up in practice.

To the surprise of many, the decision of the court was unanimous. The ruling in Plessy v. Ferguson had been used to justify institutional segregation well beyond simply having different railcars for different races.

The fight for integration in the school system began in the middle of the 1930s and was pressed by the NAACP. Initially, schools tried to improve the obviously inferior care, attention, and quality of teaching given to African American schools and students to show that the schools were equal. That was not enough; the NAACP pushed for full integration to ensure that African Americans could have the same opportunities and education as other Americans. The

NAACP argued that segregation created an inherent inequality that would persist as long as schools remained segregated.

The chief counsel for the NAACP during the case was Thurgood Marshall, who later became the first African American member of the Supreme Court. His eloquence and conviction were part of what swayed all the justices to agree with the NAACP. The Chief Justice Earl Warren went further, saying that segregation not only institutionalized inequality, it meant that African American students were given less protection under the law.

The Supreme Court released guidelines on how to implement integration a year after the landmark decision. According to the implementation guide, federal district courts were required to oversee the integration of schools "on a racially nondiscriminatory basis with all deliberate speed." This ruling was met with extreme resistance in the Southern States that had fought so hard to maintain slavery. However, they were fighting on the wrong side of history and were eventually forced to integrate all their schools.

Rise and Strength of Civil Disobedience
One of the most notable and honorable aspects of the Civil Rights Movement was that it epitomized civil disobedience in action. Even though peaceful protestors were met with violence, they remained passive and accepted the abuse as part of the plight of being African Americans.

Civil disobedience was not a new concept. It had been successfully used in India to drive the British Imperialists out. The act of civil disobedience is defined as "the active, public, conscientious breach of the law to bring about a change in law or public policy." The transcendentalist, Henry David Thoreau, coined the term in 1848, when he refused to pay poll taxes because he was an abolitionist. He argued that citizens should fight the things that they found morally reprehensible and that were inherent in the system. He would not pay a tax that perpetuated the institution of slavery.

Though civil disobedience was used around the world to prove cultures and races were not as savage or unintelligent as their oppressors claimed, the American Civil Rights Movement was one of the largest and longest sustained movements of this kind.

One thing had become clear since the end of the Civil War – the U.S. abolished slavery, but that did not mean African Americans were treated as equals with Caucasian Americans. Over time, African Americans decided that the only way to move forward was to stand up together and show they understood what it would take to gain respect and equality. They knew it would not be an easy task, many realized they were risking their lives. However, they all knew it was necessary. They could either die alone, cowering in a country that continued to deny their humanity, or they could rise together and prove their detractors wrong.

The Niagara Movement had been the start of African American fight against tyranny, but up until the 1950s, there were still too few leaders and too few people willing to rise up. Though the Southern States were the worst offenders, it was clear from nearly every facet of the nation that African Americans were not considered equals. Equality was not something that could be won by a few people working together. It would take an incredible movement so big that it could no longer be ignored.

The verdict in Brown vs. Board of Education of Topeka Kansas was the beginning of the movement. For the first time since the Civil War had ended, the U.S. Supreme Court acknowledged that segregation created an inherent inequality. It gave hope to African Americans and opened the eyes of Caucasians who had not understood the severity of the oppressive Jim Crow laws. It also let the country know it was going to be forced to respond to the institutionalized racism that it had perpetrated. Both sides were gearing up for a much longer fight, but African Americans finally had the law on their side to make serious changes.

Having won a victory through the courts, several African American leaders began to rise to the forefront of the movement. With the courts showing their awareness of the inequality, civil disobedience gained in popularity. Some of the most iconic pictures in U.S. history came from this period. African Americans were standing together against the police, politicians, and the military. They stood in peace or boycotted in peace, and did not fight back even when their adversaries turned violent. This contrast proved what African Americans had been saying for decades – they were not treated as equals and when they tried to stand up for their rights they were violently shut down. These images forced many people within the country to re-evaluate their beliefs and the current problems within the nation. It was no longer possible to deny the truth – African Americans were not treated like Americans. The movement began following the Supreme Court's decision in 1954 and lasted through the end of the 1960s.

During this time, the NAACP also retaliated with lawsuits because peaceful protests and boycotts would only go so far. The best way to force change was through a combination of civil disobedience and legal reform. When protestors were beaten, the NAACP responded with lawsuits against the government agencies that perpetrated the crimes against African Americans. With so much news coverage of the monumental events, there was no way the courts could deny that the violence was unjustified and illegal. While protestors drew media attention to the problem, some of the best legal minds fought behind the scenes. It was the legal actions that would bring about some of the greatest changes as the country was made aware that enforcing equality through the law was the only real solution to the problem.

March on Washington

One of the most memorable and largest events of the Civil Rights Movement occurred on August 28, 1963. Over 250,000 demonstrators descended on the Washington Memorial in Washington, D.C., in what is now known as the March on Washington for Jobs and Freedom. It was the single largest demonstration in U.S. history up to that point (the protest to end the Vietnam War six years later would draw nearly twice as many in the same location).

The idea for such a large demonstration began with A. Philip Randolph near the end of 1962. He wanted to bring all the civil rights leaders together to work toward both social and economic equality. However, his idea was largely ignored. Each of the Civil Rights leaders had their own goals for how they wanted the Civil Rights Movement to go, and their goals did not always coincide. Knowing that he had to get the six primary leaders of the movement to agree to participate in the march, he immediately began pressing the others. As one of the primary leaders, Randolph would need to persuade five others to join him: Roy Wilkins of the NAACP, Reverend Martin Luther King, Jr., Whitney Young, Jr., James Farmer, and John Lewis. Randolph left the coordination and organization to Bayard Rustin. The most obvious location for the African American movement to converge was where the African American culture finally found its voice after the Civil War – Harlem. Setting up the headquarters for the massive rally in the same place as the heart of the Harlem Renaissance, Rustin successfully persuaded the other leaders to join the effort. Although their specific goals were the same, it was clear to all that the best way to success was through cooperation.

It was the first major rally and demonstration in U.S. history, but the march did not only include African Americans – organizations and allies of their movement joined in the fight against inequality. In addition to the presence of some of the greatest leaders of the movement, numerous celebrities and musicians came to show their support and entertain the large crowd on the sprawling lawn of the Lincoln Memorial.

The march began at the National Mall. The participants followed a set route, ending at the Lincoln Memorial. At the memorial, the leaders of the Civil Rights Movement spoke, with one of the most famous speeches in American history ever delivered under the eyes of the Lincoln Memorial, Martin Luther King's "I Have a Dream" speech.

It would show just how successful a peaceful movement could be, and the template for this demonstration would be used repeatedly over the coming decades for other activists to stand against similar types of oppression. The Women's March of 2017 was inspired in part by the success and speeches of the first major march in the country's capital. Without this first march, it is unlikely any of the marches since then would have been possible. It was a new and innovative idea that proved that banding together to work toward one overarching goal would do far more than leaders fighting different battles alone.

Civil Rights Act of 1964

The peaceful demonstration in the nation's capital saw results the next year in the form of the Civil Rights Act of 1964. The express purpose of the march had been to highlight economic disparity and discrimination in the workplace. Congress took note of the event and reacted with a counter to the obvious discrimination hampering African American's right to improve their economic situation.

While the initial act focused on ensuring no discrimination based on race, it was expanded at the last minute to address the obvious discrimination against women. Ironically, this last-minute addition of the protection of women was considered a possible defeat of the bill as the nation agreed that employers should not be allowed to discriminate based on race or religion, but they still did not value the work of women.

Going forward, it would be illegal for any employer to discriminate in their hiring and firing processes. Section 703 (a) specifically stated it was illegal for any employer to "fail or refuse to hire or to discharge any individual, or otherwise to discriminate against any individual with respect to his compensation, terms, conditions or privileges of employment, because of such individual's race, color, religion, sex, or national origin."

The Civil Rights Act is still enforced today. It has been updated and changed over time to reflect changes in thinking within the country

The Selma March and Bloody Sunday

Following the unequivocal success of the march on Washington, the Civil Rights Movement began to organize more marches, gaining a much greater following. One of the biggest of these was the march from Selma, Alabama, meant to reach Montgomery, Alabama. This time, the march specifically highlighted the failings of the U.S. Government to follow through with the right to vote that should have been guaranteed by the 15th Amendment.

The event was held in March of 1965, meant to encourage more African Americans to vote. Unlike the march two years earlier, this one met with resistance and violence ordered by Governor George Wallace.

Martin Luther King Jr. had been awarded the Nobel Peace Prize the year before for his persistence in fighting for African American equality in a way that exemplified civil disobedience. As he continued the fight a year on March 7, King, and those who stood with him, were assaulted by the very people who were supposed to serve and protect citizens. It was a jarring and effective display of the severity of discrimination in the country. State troopers were told to prevent the marchers from reaching their destination before they got too far. Troopers carrying nightsticks, tear gas, and whips attacked the 600 people in the march. The media caught the actions and broadcast them to the nation and the rest of the world. The images from the march completely shocked the nation and the world at large. The event came to be called "Bloody Sunday" because of the unjustified violence against peaceful protesters.

Two days later, King tried again. This time the marchers were blocked, forcing them to return to their starting point. After the second failed attempt, a group of segregationists attacked the protesters, killing the Rev. James Reeb.

When Wallace tried to get the march blocked by the federal government, the U.S. District Court Judge struck down Wallace's request, insisting the march be allowed to proceed. President Lyndon Johnson addressed the nation, voicing his support of the marchers.

On March 21, the march from Selma to Montgomery began again, this time with 2,000 marchers. There would be no resistance from the state government because President Johnson had sent in the U.S. Army and Alabama National Guard to ensure the marchers reached their destination without further hindrance. Once they reached their destination, there were almost 50,000 supporters waiting for them. Several leaders spoke to those who were assembled at the state's capital, including King. After two failed attempts, the protestors had proved they would prevail through patience, nonviolence, and civil disobedience.

It took the marchers four days to reach Montgomery, but once it was over, the entire country was aware of just how much further it had to go to reach equality. It was impossible to deny that the basic rights of African Americans were still being violated, even though the Amendments guaranteeing those rights were nearly a century old.

Voting Rights Act of 1965

Congress soon reacted to the obvious display of racism and discrimination that violated the rights of African Americans in the Southern States with the passage of the *Voting Rights Act of 1965*. Congress had been trying to work on laws regarding the disenfranchised voters in those States for several years, but the violence against a group of peaceful protesters proved why it was necessary to enact new laws.

The number of murders of Civil Rights leaders and activists across the country proved that much more needed to be done. People were peacefully standing up for their rights and were being killed because of wanting those rights guaranteed. The exposure of its cruel and dark underbelly forced the nation to acknowledge that the Amendments and Reconstruction had utterly failed to provide the necessary help the former slaves and their descendants needed. It was long overdue for the country to force those who would repress African Americans to accept that they were every bit as American as those who had arrived voluntarily from Europe. They were citizens and would be afforded the same rights extended to everyone else.

The successful march from Selma to Birmingham occurred in March 1965. By the beginning of August of that same year, President Johnson signed the *Voting Rights Act* into law. The act reiterated what should have been guaranteed by the 15th Amendment, specifying that it was illegal to, in any way, hinder the rights of citizens to register to vote, or deny them the right to vote. The act also provided for special reviews of Southern States where African Americans had been disenfranchised and threatened to keep them from voting. Any changes to voting methods, means, or locations would require approval before Southern States would be allowed to enact them. If the Attorney General or U.S. District Court found the new rules, laws, or changes to be illegal or discriminatory, the rules and laws would be struck down.

The act has been updated and changed over time to protect other groups and citizens. However, during the early 21st century, there has been some faltering on the act as Congress has done much to diminish and obstruct the intent of the law. Given the events within the country at the beginning of the 21st century, it may be necessary to review just how effective the act has been and determine if something stronger is required to ensure that entire cultures, races, and religions are not further disenfranchised.

Chapter 11 – Those Who Fought for Their Inalienable Rights in a Country That Would Deny Them

Without the leaders of the Civil Rights Movement, it would have been difficult for the movement to succeed. African Americans were scrutinized for the smallest things because the government closely regulated their behavior. While the police and other law enforcement officials would punish African Americans for things like sitting in a space reserved for whites or using a white only water fountain, they did little to stop real crimes committed against African Americans. Lynching was common, and those who perpetrated the cruel murders were not arrested, let alone prosecuted. It was a truly unjust system that allowed one race to get away with murder while the other had to follow laws about where they could go and how.

Some of the most well-known U.S. historical figures emerged during this time. From the quiet bravery of Rosa Parks to the mesmerizing dignity of Reverend Martin Luther King Jr. and the fiery passion of Malcom X, the Civil Rights Movement inspired people to act in little and big ways to shine a light on the problems African Americans faced daily. Each leader brought their own enthusiasm and methods to the movement, showing that anyone could inspire change if they were brave enough to stand up for what they believed in.

Several figures stood out because they were what was needed when it was required to move the rights of African Americans forward. Sometimes they made mistakes, but often they learned from the faults and flaws in their own approach. As the movement progressed, their tactics and methods changed, but their persistence in trying to enact change never wavered. Their work would be the foundation for almost all civil disobedience and demonstrations, helping make changes for many other causes throughout modern-day America.

The Courage of Rosa Parks

Though there were many passionate and well-spoken leaders in the Civil Rights Movement, their words and actions may not have had the fertile ground it did if not for the quiet defiance of Rosa Parks. In a time when those seeking to improve the lives of African Americans were painted as troublemakers and criminals, it was nearly impossible to get people to listen to the truth. All the well-crafted stereotypes were broken by the single action taken by a middle-aged African American woman.

Born Rosa Louise McCauley in 1913 in Tuskegee, Alabama, she attended school throughout much of her childhood and teenage years until she had to take care of her ailing grandmother. One of her memories of her childhood was of the Ku Klux Klan marching through her neighborhood as her father stood with a shotgun in front of their home. From a young age, this iconic member of the Civil Rights Movement understood how the Caucasians were intimidating and disenfranchising African Americans from voting.

At 19 years old, she married Raymond Parks, and took the name that would one day be known internationally. He was already a member of the NAACP, and very quietly at first, she began to support him and the organization in their efforts to improve African American lives. Despite her involvement, she had an impeccable record and a very professional demeanor.

On 1 December 1955, Parks boarded a bus in Montgomery, Alabama. After paying for the ride, she moved toward the back of the bus and sat in the front of the section marked for African Americans. As the bus moved through the city, the white section filled up quickly. Bus drivers had the right to assign seats, but they were not allowed to force passengers to stand so that others could sit if there were no other seats available. However, that was exactly what the bus driver, James F. Blake, demanded of Rosa Parks and three other African American passengers when there were no seats for a couple of white men. He moved the African American designation sign and said that the seats were now to be given to the white men. The three other African American passengers rose and moved further back on the bus; Parks rose to let one of the men out of his seat, then sat down in his seat next to the window.

When she refused to move to accommodate the driver's new designation, he called the police, who then arrested the mild-mannered Rosa Parks. In remembering the incident, Parks responded to questions about why she did it: "I had to know, once and for all, what rights I had as a human being and a citizen of Montgomery, Alabama." In her autobiography, she elaborated on her motivations.

> People always say that I didn't give up my seat because I was tired, but that isn't true. I was not tired physically, or no more tired than I usually was at the end of a working day. I was not old, although some people have that image of me. I was forty-two. No, the only tired I was, was tired of giving in.

Her autobiography highlighted two things about the incident. First, some people tried to paint a picture of a bus driver trying to move an elderly woman. They tried to perpetuate an untruth so people would see it as a one-time event. It was as if they were trying to say the problem was the bus driver wanting an elderly woman to move, not a middle-aged woman who was sick of settling for less. This was meant to undercut her stand, but it did not work. Pictures of the quiet woman getting fingerprinted at the police station made front-page news, and drew attention from around the world. To avert this and change the narrative, Southern government leaders were trying to avoid the actual problem.

The second motive highlighted by her thoughts was that it was not troublemakers who were reaching a breaking point, so people outside of the South started to take notice. On the evening of her arrest, E.D. Nixon (the President of the NAACP Montgomery chapter) spoke with Jo Ann Robinson, a professor at Alabama State College, to determine what they could do to support Parks. Robinson was a member of the Women's Political Council, and her response to the event was to establish a boycott of the bus line.

Three days after Parks' arrest, the Montgomery Bus Boycott was announced. They were no longer willing to settle for just being allowed to remain seated. The boycotters were now ready to insist on having African American bus drivers and changing the way seating would be assigned on buses. One of the organizers of this boycott was Reverend Martin Luther King, Jr. The boycott proved to be the start of his fight for civil rights. It lasted for over a year, as African Americans found other means of getting to and from work and school so they would not have to deal with racism and unfair treatment. Despite the terrorism of segregationists who tried to intimidate African Americans into giving up (including destroying African American churches), the boycott succeeded. Faced with serious financial problems with the bus lines, segregation stopped on the buses.

When Parks was found guilty of the charges against her, she appealed the ruling. Before her case went further, the US District Court for the region, made a ruling on the constitutionality of segregation on the bus in another case, *Browder v. Gayle*. It ruled that segregation on public buses was unconstitutional, which the US Supreme Court upheld in 1956.

Rosa Parks succeeded where others didn't because of her unimpeachable character and reputation. As soon as she stood up for their rights, it became impossible to wave away the problems of segregation as being something that most African Americans accepted. She lived another 50 years after the incident, continuing to inspire and quietly advocate for what was right. She was awarded numerous honors for her courage over the years. Parks died in October of 2005, as one of the most well-recognized figures of the Civil Rights Era.

The Dream of Martin Luther King

A larger than life figure, Reverend Martin Luther King, Jr. had humble beginnings. Born in 1929 in Atlanta, Georgia, he was the child of a minister, which helped shape the person he would become as an adult. Though his father fought racism where he could, he tried to shield his children from the dangers and problems inherent in the system.

King himself was a troublemaker as a child. He had snuck out of his home to watch a parade after his grandmother died. Feeling guilty about having done so, he jumped out of a window of the family's second story home. His behavior improved as he grew older, and he would skip two grades in high school, entering Morehouse College when he was only 15. Popular even in college, he originally was not interested in religion and politics. It was only during his junior year at Morehouse that King began to be interested in religion, on his own terms. This did not mean that he agreed with his father's conservative leanings.

It was under the mentoring of Benjamin E. Mays that King began to take an interest in fighting for racial equality. He worked toward his doctorate in Boston, where he met his future wife, Coretta Scott. King was still working on his dissertation when he accepted the position of Pastor in Montgomery, Alabama. He was 25 years old in 1955 when he finally earned his doctorate degree. By this time, he was already working with the NAACP to fight segregation and inequality. In December of that year, King began to build the legacy that would make him one of the most recognizable people in U.S. history.

After Rosa Parks gave the NAACP the case they needed to start pressing for reform, King stepped to the forefront and began coordinating the bus boycott. An eloquent speaker with an impressive education, people listened to this new face of the Civil Rights Movement. King would go on to help make numerous events successful. From the demonstration in Washington, D.C., to the March from Selma to Montgomery, King was a major player in the movement. His presence and dedication to the cause inspired others to take chances they likely would not have taken without such a strong leader.

As one of the most well-known faces of the movement, King knew his life was in constant peril. Nor was this the only way in which his life would be challenged. Governments in Southern States and several federal government agencies constantly smeared his name and tried to undermine his reputation. However, nothing they did deterred him from his mission of bringing equality to African Americans. His speeches and letters, particularly his "I Have a Dream" speech, are some of the most famous works of U.S. literature.

Though he was dedicated to nonviolence, those he fought against were not averse to it. On 3 April 1968, he gave his last speech, known as his "I've Been to the Mountaintop" speech, to a crowd in Memphis, Tennessee. He told them "I've seen the promised land. I may not get there with you. But I want you to know tonight that we, as a people, will get to the promised land." The next day he was assassinated by James Earl Ray.

Today, King is the only American not a President to have a federal holiday in his honor. His legacy has been carried on over the years, and much of his message has been watered down to suit different narratives. Still, he was an outspoken proponent against numerous injustices, including being openly against the Vietnam War. Though he was flawed (information on his extra-marital affairs were released as part of the *Freedom of Information Act*), his willingness to risk his life for what he thought was right was undeniable. His legacy proves that no person, no hero is perfect. However, it is possible to still fight for what is right. Despite his flaws, King was willing to sacrifice everything for the causes that he believed in.

The Trials and Change of Heart of Malcolm X

Malcolm X was unlike any of the other figures in the Civil Rights Movement. While many of the leaders came from the Deep South, Malcolm Little was born in Omaha, Nebraska, in May of 1925, as one of eight children. Like King, he was the son of an outspoken minister. Unlike King's father, Little's father was a supporter of the teachings of Marcus Garvey. This unpopular stance with segregationists and white supremacists led to frequent threats to the Little family, resulting in them moving twice before the young Civil Rights leader was four years old. Despite trying to escape the threats, the family's home in Lansing, Michigan was burned down in 1929. Earl Little, Malcolm Little's father, was found dead in 1931. Both the arson and murder accounts were ignored, with the law enforcement officials calling both tragedies accidents.

Because of the incidents, Louise Little, Malcolm Little's mother, suffered mental trauma. A few years after the death of her husband, she was committed to a mental institution. Her children were sent to relatives and orphanages. Having spent most of his early life surrounded by misfortune because of his family's skin color and beliefs, Malcolm was less willing to negotiate with the terrorists who had destroyed his family.

By 1946, Little was living in Boston, where he and a friend were arrested on burglary charges. He would serve seven of the ten years he was sentenced to. During this time, Malcolm began to reflect on his life and decided to further his education. Inspired by his brother, Reginald, he converted to being a Muslim.

He joined the Nation of Islam, and studied under Elijah Muhammad. Muhammad taught that Caucasians worked to keep African Americans in a state of inequality. Because his father believed in the teachings of Garvey, Malcolm would come to believe that African Americans would need to find their own way in a place away from the white people who oppressed them. By the time he was released from prison in 1952, Malcolm had changed his surname to the one by which he is known today – Malcolm X. He said that Little was the name that was given to his family while they were in slavery, and he would not continue to use it. Since there was no record of what his family's name was originally, he chose X to show that his history was lost because of the oppression of the U.S.

Despite his criminal record, Malcolm X was a gifted, intelligent, and charismatic figure. He denied the teachings of Christians who had used their religion to justify, first slavery, and then the treatment of African Americans as lesser citizens. As a result, Malcolm X was tasked with helping to establish mosques around the country, notably in Detroit and Harlem. His appeal attracted a far greater number of people than anticipated. Because of the way he articulated the beliefs of his religion and the potential for the future, the members of the Nation of Islam grew from 500 to more than 30,000 between 1952 and 1963.

However, his words and actions were not part of the civil disobedience carried out by so many others during the Civil Rights Movement. In 1959, he appeared on a TV show with Mike Wallace. The special lasted for a week and was titled *The Hate That Hate Produced*. Once it was over, X had not only become the face of the Islamic African American Movement, he had come to the attention of the federal government. The FBI began to track and monitor him, from a distance at first, then infiltrating his inner circle. They bugged the locations where he was and conducted wiretaps on X.

A staunch believer in his religion, X was devastated to learn that his mentor had committed adultery with roughly half a dozen women, even having children through those affairs. Having abstained until his own marriage, X refused to assist in the cover-up of his mentor's misdeeds. It also shook his belief in the organization that he had helped build over a decade.

In 1964, he founded his own organization, the Muslim Mosque, Inc., and took a pilgrimage to Mecca. On his travels abroad, he found the things he had believed for so long could be overcome – that integration was possible when people's hearts and minds were touched. This was a result of his positive encounters with "blond-haired, blue-eyed men I could call my brothers," according to X. Upon his return, his message was to the American people, not just African Americans.

Malcolm X's home was firebombed in 1965. The following week, three assassins shot him 15 times onstage at the Manhattan's Audubon Ballroom. He died before reaching the hospital. More than 1,000 people attended his funeral, even insisting on burying their friend themselves. The following year, the three assassins faced charges of first-degree murder and were found guilty.

The Calm Dignity of Dorothy Height

Although Rosa Parks is the most famous woman in the Civil Rights Movement, her actions on December 1, 1955, might not have had nearly the impact they had if not for the efforts of Dorothy Height. Unlike many of the other Civil Rights leaders who focused on equality for African Americans, Height focused on rights for women. Because the two causes had roots in many of the same problems and discrimination, Height often worked with Civil Rights leaders to forward the rights of women.

Height was born in Richmond, Virginia, in 1912. She was still young when her family moved to Pennsylvania where she went to an integrated school. By high school, she had proved she was a talented speaker, attracting a lot of attention when she competed and won on a national level. Her initial acceptance at Barnard College was rescinded when the college decided they had met the requisite number of African American students, ignoring her qualifications as an outstanding student. New York University accepted her, and she went on to earn her bachelor's and master's degrees there.

After college, she became a social worker until 1937 when she joined the Harlem YWCA. While working there, she met Mary McLeod Bethune, one of the founders of the National Council of Negro Women, and Eleanor Roosevelt. Following the meeting, Height became friends with Bethune and joined her council. She was instrumental in the integration of the YWCA in 1946, and was one of the people to establish the Center for Racial Justice in 1965. She led the Center until 1977.

Height worked with the leader of the Montgomery chapter of the NAACP to ensure the Montgomery public transportation center faced civil repercussions for their illegal and unethical treatment of African Americans. She began the organization of a boycott. From this event, she would become instrumental in the Civil Rights Movement, more behind the scenes rather than its public face. While there were six men who stood at the front for the moment, much of their achievements would have been difficult or non-existent without Height. She was one of the primary organizers of the March on Washington, standing beside King when he gave his infamous speech.

One of the things she noticed during the march was that the males were more than happy to have female support, but they did not give women a say. Despite her exceptional speaking skills, Height was not invited to speak, with her position being a silent figure beside the men. By 1971, her focus turned from helping establish the rights for African Americans to working for the rights and equality of all women. She was one of the founding members of the National Women's Political Caucus, even as she continued to lead the YWCA.

Over the next few decades, almost every American President would recognize her, even Bill Clinton. To Height the question of equality should have been universal, not broken up based on race or gender. Without equality for everyone, there wouldn't be equality for anyone. She died on April 20, 2010. Many politicians and political proponents who had fought alongside her in both the Civil Rights Movement and to further the rights of women attended her funeral.

The Appointment of Justice Thurgood Marshall

Thurgood Marshall was first a defender of equal rights for African Americans, then he became the face of what they could become if they continued to press for equal rights. Born in 1908 in Baltimore, Maryland, Thurgood Marshall would go on to become one of the largest figures behind the scenes of the Civil Rights Movement.

He was always an exemplary student who performed well and could win arguments against members of his debate team. While his grades and academic achievements were impressive, he was not without his flaws. He was a high school student who became well known for memorizing the U.S. Constitution. What was less known was he was forced to memorize it as punishment for causing trouble.

He attended Lincoln University and joined what would turn out to be one of the most influential student bodies in the African American community. His peers included Langston Hughes, Cab Calloway (a highly influential jazz musician), and Kwame Nkrumah (who would later become the President of Ghana).

Having graduated from Lincoln University with honors, any school would be lucky to have Marshall as a law student. However, the University of Maryland Law School declined his application purely based on his race (even though he was overqualified for their legal program). This highlighted just how much work he had in front of him to ensure the laws were upheld – a school was ignoring qualifications and discriminating purely based on race. Howard University in Washington, D.C., accepted him, and that was when he began his work toward ensuring civil rights, long before the Civil Rights Movement began. In 1933, he graduated magna cum laude.

After unsuccessfully trying to found his own practice in Baltimore (lack of experience made it difficult for him to attract clients), it became clear he needed another choice, so he became a legal counsel for the NAACP. One of his first cases mirrored his own experience with colleges in the U.S. – Murray vs. Pearson focused on the denial of a student based on his race instead of academic qualifications. It was one of his first major victories, occurring just three years after he graduated from law school. Later that year, he moved to New York City to work for the NAACP full-time. There he flourished and became one of the most successful and well-known attorneys.

In 1940, he spoke in front of the U.S. Supreme Court for Chambers vs. Florida. His first appearance was a winning case as he proved the police coerced the murder confession. Perhaps his biggest case was Brown vs. Board of Education of Topeka Kansas, which he helped to win for the NAACP, making him one of the earliest proponents of the Civil Rights Movement.

Marshall earned a title in 1961 that had never been held by an African American – as a justice on the U.S. Second Circuit Court of Appeals, appointed by President John F. Kennedy. Four years later he was given an even more prominent position as the U.S. Solicitor general, appointed by President Lyndon B. Johnson. During his time as the solicitor general, he won 14 of his 19 cases. In 1967, he was given one of the most prominent positions in the U.S. – he was named a Supreme Court Justice, again earning his appointment through President Johnson.

Marshall was a justice of the highest U.S. court for nearly a quarter of a century. In 1991, he retired and was replaced by the conservative Justice Clarence Thomas. Marshall died in 1993, just two years after retiring. He had one of the longest careers of fighting for equality in U.S. history, and earned his place alongside Parks, King, and others as a primary figure of the Civil Rights Movement.

The Peaceful Perseverance of Representative John Lewis

Though there were many people who influenced the movement, only a small handful had such a long and influential career as John Lewis. Considered one of the six biggest influencers of the Civil Rights Movement, he continues to fight for equality today, meaning that nearly his entire life has been spent fighting for equality.

Born in 1940 in Troy, Alabama, he led a relatively quiet life, attending a segregated school as an average student. He was still very young when the Montgomery Bus Boycott spurred him to action. He heard the words of King and wanted to join the cause, igniting a fire in him that would last for decades.

He attended Fisk University in Nashville, Tennessee. There he held his first organized sit-in over the segregation of lunch counters. He would also voluntarily join the Freedom Rides. These rides were a way of protesting the interstate bus segregation that spanned the Southern States. It was required that participants sit in "white only" seats, an act that got several protestors killed. Lewis was beaten and arrested for his stance and the role he played in the Freedom Rides.

He became the chairman of the Student Nonviolent Coordinating Committee in 1961 and served in this role until 1966. At the young age of 23, he was named one of the six primary leaders of the Civil Rights Movement, making him the youngest member. He would go on to march beside King during the first attempt to march from Selma to Montgomery. Over the years, Lewis was arrested over 40 times and severely beaten by law enforcement officers, yet was never deterred in the fight for equality.

In 1966, he stepped down from the chairmanship of the Student Nonviolent Coordinating Committee and was appointed to serve as the Associate Director to the Field Foundation. He also worked to assist in getting more African American voters through the Southern Regional Council's voter registration program. President Jimmy Carter appointed him to be the director and manager of the volunteers of ACTION Agency, an agency of volunteers around the country.

Having served in many different councils and organizations, Lewis finally made the switch to being a full-time politician in 1981 when he became a member of the Atlanta City Council. It was the first time he was elected to a position, instead of being appointed or volunteering. In 1986, he ran for and won a seat as a representative in the House of Representatives. He still serves in this position today.

Over the years, he has earned numerous awards and recognition for his efforts. Since he was young at the beginning of the Civil Rights Movement, he is the only surviving member of the most notable figures. The lasting impression of the works of King, Parks, and others who were willing to fight, lives on in Lewis. In Congress, he still advocates for equality for everyone, from race to gender to social status.

Conclusion

The end of the Civil War was the beginning of an entirely different struggle for the former slaves who were freed at the end of the bloody conflict. Though they were no longer slaves, the areas of the United States where African Americans had been enslaved were hostile toward them and their former masters quickly implemented as many methods of oppression as they could. The passage of new Amendments and federal assistance did nothing to dissuade the Southern States from enacting cruel and discriminatory laws that undermined the rights of African Americans. Nor did the Northern States do much to help those who had escaped slavery before the war, having nothing with which to rebuild their lives. The hypocrisy was obvious, although not often addressed.

African Americans were initially submissive to the situations because they had been slaves and were accustomed to oppression. Over the next few decades, they would begin to realize that things were only marginally better, as they sought to improve their situation. Some saw hope in the form of leaving the places where they had been born and enslaved. The result was a mass migration to Kansas, largely through the help of a couple of African Americans who were willing to share their leadership skills and talents to improve the lives of others.

Those who were either unwilling or unable to leave their homes began to express themselves through various types of art. The

Harlem Renaissance demonstrated African Americans had their own culture and the expression of that culture was beginning to flourish despite harsh conditions around the country. Paintings and drawings emerged in vibrant colors that showed the uncertainty and unhappiness of many African Americans. It proved they could overcome and find the lighter aspects of life regardless of the conditions. It portrayed a hope for, and belief in, a better future that was felt by the artists, and an unwillingness to let circumstance bring them down.

Even more startling was the fictional, biographical, and musical works that came from the Harlem Renaissance. Those who had the ability to write and play music could translate the African American experience into something that caught the attention of the entire nation and spread across the world. Langston Hughes was sought as a poet among many Caucasian institutions. Louis Armstrong and Ella Fitzgerald became two of the most well-respected and popular musicians in the 20th century. The writers and musicians helped to begin the breakdown of Jim Crow laws, even though the law was only ignored for a few select individuals. Jackie Robinson was the first African American to really press for equality. His courage and talent in the sport of baseball helped to prove that African Americans were not the stereotyped people the media and politicians tried to portray them as.

The lasting effects of jazz as a genre not only created the bedrock for numerous other types of music; it also opened the eyes of the country and the world to the inherent talent of African Americas even in adversity. The music spoke to people on a level that most other genres didn't. The upbeat nature of the genre reflected the hope that African Americans had for themselves even when the lyrics were sad. It provided a new foundation for the African American experience in a universal language. It exemplified the creativity and emotion of an oppressed people.

However, the biggest changes began in the 1950s with the Civil Rights Movement, and it would continue until the end of the 1960s. Both likely and unlikely leaders began to stand up for African American rights. At first many of the steps that were taken were small. When it became clear they could not wait for the federal government to step in and help, several leaders rose up to press for the rights of African Americans. Knowing they were risking their lives, these leaders showed they would no longer be intimidated into allowing the inequality to persist any longer.

While a lot of changes were implemented, the problem was still not solved by the end of the 1960s. However, the movement made it clear that African Americans were willing to fight for the rights that should have been guaranteed them. They were no longer willing to be treated as second-class citizens. They had learned how best to fight within a system that often failed to protect them, proving that change was possible.

Preview of World War 2
A Captivating Guide from Beginning to End

Introduction

The Second World War was one of the most traumatic events in human history. Across the world, existing conflicts became connected, entangling nations in a vast web of violence. It was fought on land, sea, and air, touching every inhabited continent. Over 55 million people died, some of them combatants, some civilians caught up in the violence, and some murdered by their own governments.

It was the war that unleashed the Holocaust and the atomic bomb upon the world. But it was also a war that featured acts of courage and self-sacrifice on every side.

The world would never be the same again.

Chapter 1 – The Rising Tide

The Second World War grew out of conflicts in two parts of the world: Europe and East Asia. Though the two would eventually become entangled, it's easier to understand the causes of the war by looking at them separately.

Europe's problems were rooted in centuries of competition between powerful nations crammed together on a small and densely populated continent. Most of the world's toughest, most stubborn, and most ambitious kids were crammed together in a single small playground. Conflict was all but inevitable.

The most recent large European conflict had been the First World War. This was the first industrialized war, a hugely traumatic event for all the participants. In the aftermath, Germany was severely punished for its aggression by the victorious Allied powers. The remains of the Austro-Hungarian empire fell apart, creating instability in the east. And the Russian Empire, whose government had been overthrown during the turmoil of the war, became the Union of Soviet Socialist Republics (USSR), the first global power to adopt the new ideology of communism.

From this situation of instability, a new form of politics emerged. Across Europe, extreme right-wing parties adopted ultranationalistic views. Many of them incorporated ideas of racial superiority. Most were strongly influenced by the fear of communism. All relied on scapegoating outsiders to make themselves more powerful.

The first to reach prominence was the Fascist Party in Italy under Benito Mussolini. Mussolini was a veteran soldier, gifted orator, and skilled administrator. He rallied disenchanted left-wingers and those who felt put down by corrupt politicians and forceful trade unions. Using a mixture of persuasion and intimidation, he won the 1922 election and became prime minister. Through a series of laws, he turned his country into a one-party dictatorship. Most of his achievements were domestic, bringing order and efficiency at the price of freedom, but he also had ambitions abroad. He wanted Italy to be a colonial power like Britain or France, and so in 1935-6 his forces conquered Abyssinia.

Mussolini was surpassed in almost every way by the man who reached power in Germany a decade later—Adolph Hitler. A decorated veteran of the First World War, Hitler was embittered at the Versailles Treaty, which imposed crushing restrictions upon Germany in the aftermath of the war. He developed a monstrous ideology that combined racism, homophobia, and a bitter hatred of communism. Like Mussolini, he brought together oratory and street violence to seize control of Germany. Once elected chancellor in 1933, he purged all opposition and had himself made Führer, the nation's "leader" or "guide." He then escalated the rearmament of Germany, casting off the shackles of Versailles.

Hitler and Mussolini intervened in the Spanish Civil War of 1936-9. Rather than have their nations join the war, they sent parts of their armed forces to support Franco's right-wing armies, testing new military technology and tactics while ensuring the victory of a man they expected to be an ally—a man who would in fact keep his nation out of the coming war for Europe.

Meanwhile, Hitler was playing a game of chicken with the other European powers. In March 1936, he occupied the Rhineland, a part of Germany that had been demilitarized after the war. Two years later, he annexed his own homeland of Austria, with its large German-speaking population. He occupied parts of Czechoslovakia that fall and finished the job off the following spring. At every turn, the rest of Europe backed down rather than go to war to protect less powerful nations.

Meanwhile, in Asia, the Chinese revolutions of 1911 and 1913, along with the Chinese Civil War that broke out in 1927, had triggered a parallel period of instability. Nationalists and communists battled for control of a vast nation, destroying the regional balance of power.

Japan was a nation on the rise. Economic growth had created a sense of ambition which had then been threatened by a downturn in the 1930s. Interventions by Western powers, including their colonies in Asia and a restrictive naval treaty of 1930, embittered many in Japan, who saw the Europeans and Americans as colonialist outsiders meddling in their part of the world.

The Japanese began a period of expansion, looking to increase their political dominance and their control of valuable raw resources. They invaded Chinese Manchuria in 1931 and from then on kept encroaching on Chinese territory. At last, in 1937, the Chinese nationalist leader Chiang Kai-Shek gave up on his previous policy of giving ground to buy himself time. A minor skirmish escalated into the Second Sino-Japanese War.

From an Asian point of view, the war had already begun. But it would be Hitler who pushed Europe over the brink and gave the war its Western start date of 1939.

Chapter 2 – From Poland to the Fall of France

Hitler had long looked at Poland with hungry eyes. He believed in the racial superiority of Germans and wanted more space for them to live in. Poland, just over the border to the east, was perfect. Many Nazi supporters had fought against Polish incursions following the First World War, and so they were already primed for conflict with the Poles.

On September 1, 1939, German troops swept across the Polish border. It was a war the Germans had long been preparing for. Under the secret terms of the Molotov-Ribbentrop Pact, Germany and the USSR had agreed not only to keep the peace between themselves but to partition Poland between them. Meanwhile, German forces had been gathering on the Polish border.

Fifty-five German divisions swept into Poland. These were primarily tanks and motorized infantry, allowing them to advance swiftly. The Luftwaffe, the German air force, pounded the Polish defenses. With only 17 divisions at the front and 22 more preparing, the Poles were vastly outnumbered. It was the same in the air, where 4,700 modern German planes faced the 842 outdated aircraft of the Polish air force.

On top of this, some German troops were already experienced soldiers, veterans of the fighting in Spain.

This was the first example of what came to be called Blitzkrieg— "lightning war." German commanders such as Heinz Guderian had long been advocating such a fast-paced, hard-hitting form of warfare. The open plains of Poland were the perfect place to showcase what they could do.

The Germans advanced 140 miles in the first week, reaching the borders of Warsaw. There, at the Polish capital, some of the fiercest fighting took place.

On September 17, the Russians invaded Poland from the east. Most of the Polish forces had already been smashed by the Germans. The following day, the Polish high command fled into exile. Eighty thousand soldiers followed them, fleeing to France and Britain. The Warsaw garrison surrendered on September 28, the last substantial Polish forces on October 5.

The Poles had powerful allies. They had had a treaty with France since 1921 and one with Britain since 1939. On September 3, Britain and France declared war on Germany. Australia, Canada, New Zealand, and South Africa, all independent dominions within the British Commonwealth, followed their parent country's lead. But none of them were close enough to help as Poland was engulfed.

The months that followed are often referred to as the "phony war" due to the lack of direct conflict between the major belligerents. But this hides the frantic activity going on across Europe.

While the invasion of Poland was still underway, the French made a brief and half-hearted attempt to invade the German Saarland, only to run up against the carefully prepared defenses of the Siegfried Line.

In the east, the USSR began swallowing up territory not yet occupied by the Germans. This included a grueling invasion of Finland, known as the Winter War, in which poorly prepared Soviet troops became bogged down in bitter cold that stopped vehicles from working and froze men to death. Though the Russians gained territory from the Finns, it was in many ways a Pyrrhic victory.

The Allies began a naval blockade of Germany. The power of the British Royal Navy gave them a huge advantage. The Germans countered with submarines, known as U-boats, which slipped out into the Atlantic to attack convoys bringing vital war supplies to Britain and France. These supplies included equipment hastily ordered from the Americans, who were happy to play a profitable part in bolstering friendly nations without entangling themselves in a European war.

Meanwhile, Polish troops arrived in Britain and France. They brought with them cryptographers who had begun work on breaking the Enigma code, used for Germany's highest-level military communications. This fed into the work of British military intelligence, which in a matter of months was turned from a neglected corner of government into the world's leading organization for covert information gathering and analysis.

In April 1940, Germany invaded Denmark and Norway to protect shipping routes for vital iron ore from Sweden. British, French, and Polish troops rushed to support the Norwegians. But once again, the Germans swiftly overwhelmed their opponents.

One important result of the failure in Norway was a change of government in Britain. On May 10, 1940, Winston Churchill replaced Neville Chamberlain as prime minister. Churchill, long a belligerent and divisive figure in British politics, formed a coalition government that united the country for war. His strong leadership would prove vital in the days ahead.

Just as Churchill was taking up his new role, Germany was preparing for its most dramatic success of the war—the invasion of France. As forces gathered on the western border over the winter, the German army had adopted a revised plan of action developed by Field Marshal Erich von Manstein. Manstein's plan shifted the focus of the German offensive south, so that the main strike would come through the Ardennes forest, a region supposedly impassable to a modern army. That change of plan proved critical.

One hundred and thirty-six German army divisions had been gathered for the invasion. Facing them were 94 French, 22 Belgian, and 10 British divisions. The Germans had fewer tanks than their opponents, but the superior quality of those tanks and the skill of tank commanders such as Guderian and Erwin Rommel would give the Germans the advantage in armored forces.

On May 10, 1940, the Germans launched their attack.

In the Netherlands, the Dutch army was swiftly overwhelmed by the forces of their more powerful neighbor. The Dutch surrendered after only four days of fighting.

In Belgium, the attack began with the arrival of German paratroopers on the roof of the massive concrete fort at Eben Emael, part of a defensive system along the Albert Canal. The paratroopers destroyed the gun turrets and defeated a garrison that outnumbered them more than ten to one. With the Belgian defensive line weakened, its armies outnumbered, and half the air force quickly destroyed, the nation was swiftly overrun with German troops.

At the southern end of the advance, German Panzer divisions—fast-moving units consisting of tanks and their supporting troops—raced through the Ardennes in southern Belgium and burst into France. The French had not been prepared for an attack in this area and so the Germans hit them at the point where two of their weakest armies joined. The Germans quickly broke through, fought their way across the River Meuse, and then raced northwest. On May 20, they reached the English Channel, splitting the Allied forces in half.

The British Expeditionary Force, along with French and other Allied troops, were surrounded on a shrinking patch of ground. On May 26, the British began evacuating these beleaguered troops through the port of Dunkirk, while a French rearguard held off the Germans; 338,000 men, including 120,000 French, were evacuated. Their survival was vital to maintaining the Allied war effort and helped to boost morale back in Britain, but some in France saw this as a betrayal, abandoning them in their hour of need.

With the Channel coast clear, the Germans swept south, surrounding the bulk of the remaining French troops. Many of the French were stationed on the Maginot Line, a system of concrete fortresses that the Germans had simply bypassed with their Ardennes offensive. Once again, the French were outmaneuvered and overwhelmed.

The French, militarily beaten, surrendered on June 22. The country was divided. The north and west were occupied by the Germans. The southeast became a puppet state under the right-wing Vichy regime.

Meanwhile, on June 10, Mussolini sent troops across the Alps into southeastern France. It was a token effort to claim some glory and territory before Hitler got it all. More importantly, it brought Italy into the war.

Check out this book!

Preview of Haitian Revolution

A Captivating Guide to the Abolition of Slavery

Introduction

The revolutions of the late 18th century and early 19th century were fought all over the western world. From America to France to Saint-Domingue, all of the revolutionaries sought the same thing— independence from tyranny. However, the tyranny confronted by the different revolutionaries was different. On the small island of Saint-Domingue, the tyrants were the slave owners, people who not only denied them freedom, but felt justified in killing their slaves. It was the first and only time that a slave rebellion resulted in a new state.

Known today as the Haitian Revolution, the success of the slave rebellion began to change the way slaves were viewed. Although it took nearly another 100 years to eradicate slavery in the west, the parallels between what the Americans and French had done to the slaves was impossible to ignore.

Even though the former slaves of Saint-Domingue were able to achieve some level of freedom before the turn of the century, the interference by other European countries kept the island bathed in blood until 1804. Nearly a decade passed between the initial slave rebellion and the final massacre that forced other countries to recognize Haitian independence.

Chapter 1: The Wealth from Saint-Domingue

Saint-Domingue covered the entire island. Prior to the Treaty of Ryswick that was made in 1697, the island had been a Spanish colony called Hispaniola. Following the treaty, the Spanish recognized France's claim on the western third of the island. The French had occupied this portion of the island for most of the century, so their system was already established by the time they were considered the rightful owners of the territory. This was part of the reason for the booming success of the territory that came to be known as Saint-Domingue.

Over the next 100 years, the French brought in approximately 800,000 slaves from Africa. The colonists quickly turned to cruel and torturous methods of intimidating their new slaves. As the French turned to increasingly more barbaric methods of controlling their slaves, their slaves became increasingly desperate for change. Most of the 18th century saw small revolts and conspiracies that sought to establish small pockets of freedom. These failed largely because the slaves were not as organized as the slave holders.

As colonists felt they had adequate control over their slaves, they were able to turn the fertile lands into a highly profitable colony for France. Before the Slave Rebellion of 1791, the French colony of Saint-Domingue shared the status of top sugar exporter in the world with Jamaica. As a result of the increasing prosperity and potential of the small island, the capital was moved to the port tow Port-au-Prince on the western side of the island. This allowed for a better flow of transportation and slaves to and from the island.

While sugar was the top export from most of the Caribbean islands, Saint-Domingue was also a source of other high-value exports, particularly coffee and cotton. The rich soil and generally favorable environment for growing crops made it ideal for growing a wide range of products that were difficult to grow on other continents.

However, the agricultural boom had several detrimental factors that helped set up a society that could not be perpetuated. The high demand for labor to retain the status as a jewel among colonies was done on the backs of countless slaves. As one of the most profitable colonies, and certainly the most profitable of the French colonies, the idea of freeing the slaves was not something that the monarchy would consider.

The cruelty and refusal to recognize the humanity of the slaves coupled with the extreme imbalance in the slave-to-colonist ratio resulted in King Louis the XIV becoming so distressed by the savage abuse of the slaves that he enacted the Code Noir in 1685. The code was meant to keep slave owners from the worst kinds of violence that had started to become prevalent at the time. Even though the slaves were considered property, Louis XIV did not see the brutality of the colonists as being justified, or morally acceptable.

Despite the Code Noir, slave owners felt justified that their actions were vindicated by the potential threat of a slave rebellion. Over the next 100 years, their violent treatment of the slaves only grew worse.

Guillaume Raynal was one of the most vocal about the inevitability of an uprising because of the inhumane cruelty of the colonists. As one of the most revered French Enlightenment philosophers of his time, Raynal understood that the slaves were humans who would only endure so much before they would reach a breaking point. He issued a prophetic warning more than ten years before the famous French Declaration of the Rights of Man and of the Citizen:

"The Africans only want a chief, sufficiently courageous, to lead them on to vengeance and slaughter." While the French were able to see their own oppression under the French monarchy, they could not extend the same ideology to the slaves that they oppressed and abused. The only part of Raynal's warning that the colonists heeded was the threat of the unified slaves. Instead of modifying their behaviors for the better, the slave masters became crueler, seeking to break the spirits of their slaves. Instead of creating the desired abject fear of their masters, this increased brutality created a greater sense of resolve and rebellion within the slaves.

As Raynal predicted, the slaves would rebel. However, the irony behind the rebellion was that it was triggered by the French Revolution. The ideals and espoused beliefs of the French Revolution resonated with the slaves, but it was the brutality of the oppressed French population under the monarchy that seems to have inspired the slaves into creating a strategic rebellion.

Check out this book!

Make sure to check out Captivating history to see more of our books

If you're interested in mythology books, please check out Matt Clayton

Bibliography

"The Legacy of Slave Songs in the United States and Brazil: Musical Dialogues in the Post-emancipation Period," M. Abreu.

Black History Milestones,

BlackPast.org

Britannica.com.

Civil War Trust: John Brown.

Documenting the American South,

E2BN - East of England Broadband Network and MLA East of England

Encyclopædia Britannica

Fighting…Maybe for Freedom, but Probably Not, History.org.

Fighting…Maybe for Freedom, but Probably Not, History.org.

Lucy Terry Prince,

Nat Turner, History.com.

National Museum of African American History & Culture,

Office of the Historian: The Amistad Case, 1839.

Phillis Wheatley; an Eighteenth-century Genius in Bondage,

Plantation Culture,

Slave Experience, PBS.

The Abolition Project,

The Slave Experience; Education, Art, & Culture,

US History – Pre-Columbian to the New Millennium, USHistory.org.

Singing in Slavery: Songs of Survival, Songs of Freedom, PBS.org.

14th Amendment, Cornell Law School

15th Amendment, Cornell Law School

About Dr. King, The King Center

Black Codes, NYCLU

Blacks in the Military, Elissa Haney, infoplease Sandbox Network Inc

Booker Taliaferro Washington, infoplease, Sandbox Network Inc

Brown V. Board of Education, History.com

Civil Rights Movement, History.com

Congressman John Lewis Representing Georgia's 5th District, Bibliography.

Dorothy Height, Biography, A&E Television Networks

Ella Fitzgerald, Universal Music Enterprise

Exodus to Kansas, Damari Davis, National Archives

George Washington Carver, History.com

Harlem Renaissance, History.com

Hiram Rhodes Revels, History, Art & Archives

History of Federal Voting Rights Laws, Department of Justice

Howard University, Erica L. Taylor, Little Known History Fact: HU, blAckamerciaweb.com

http://www.thekingcenter.org/archive/theme/4733, The King Center

https://www.biography.com/people/martin-luther-king-jr-9365086, Biography, A&E Television Networks

Jackie Robinson,

https://www.biography.com/people/jackie-robinson-9460813, A&E Television Networks

Langston Hughes, Academy of Poets

Nora Neale Hurston, Official Site of Nora Hurston

https://www.biography.com/people/zora-neale-hurston-9347659, A&E Television Networks

Louis Armstrong – Singer, Trumpet Player, A&E Television Networks

Malcolm X, Malcom X Biography

Marcus Garvey and the Universal Negro Improvement Association, David Van Leeuwen, Teachers Serve

NAACP, Oldest and Boldest, NAACP

Niagara Movement, BlackPast.org

Official Program for the March on Washington (1963), ourdocuments.gov

Plessy V. Ferguson, History.com

Reconstruction Ends, infoplease, Sandbox Network Inc

Rosa Parks Biography, Biography online

Selma to Montgomery March, History.com

Spellman College: History in Brief, Spelman College

The Civil Rights Act of 1964 and the Equal Employment Opportunity Commission, National Archives

The Roots of Jazz, All About Jazz

The Woman with the Violin, National Museum of African American History and Culture

Thurgood Marshall Biography.com, Judge, Civil Rights Activist, Supreme Court Justice, Lawyer (1908-1993), A&E Television Networks

ABOUT CAPTIVATING HISTORY

A lot of history books just contain dry facts that will eventually bore the reader. That's why Captivating History was created. Now you can enjoy history books that will mesmerize you. But be careful though, hours can fly by, and before you know it; you're up reading way past bedtime.

Get your first history book for free here:
http://www.captivatinghistory.com/ebook

Make sure to follow us on Twitter: @CaptivHistory and Facebook: www.facebook.com/captivatinghistory so you can get all of our updates!

Free Bonus from Captivating History (Available for a Limited time)

Hi History Lovers!

Now you have a chance to join our exclusive history list so you can get your first history ebook for free as well as discounts and a potential to get more history books for free! Simply visit the link below to join.

Captivatinghistory.com/ebook

Also, make sure to follow us on:

Twitter: @Captivhistory

Facebook: Captivating History: @captivatinghistory

Printed in Great Britain
by Amazon